FOUNDATIC

ASTROLOGICAL CHART

*

With Complete Mathematics

*

By IVY M. GOLDSTEIN-JACOBSON

*

Member of:

AMERICAN FEDERATION OF ASTROLOGERS

and

FIRST TEMPLE & COLLEGE OF ASTROLOGY

AT LOS ANGELES

———————

All engravings by Marge J. Zander

Dedicated to

my beloved second mother

Maria Teolinda Oatridge

Table of Contents

Subject — Page

Our Solar System 1,
  The Celestial Equator 3,72
  The Ecliptic 3, 6,72
  Obliquity of the Ecliptic 3,72

The Basic Wheel 2, 6, 7
  Meridian, Midheaven, Zenith & Nadir 2,
  Horizon, Ascendant & Descendant 2,
  Directions North, South, East & West 2,
  Equinoxes & Solstices 6, 7
  Geographical Latitude 8,
  Geographical Longitude 9,10
  The Prime Meridians 9,10,11
  The Local Meridians 10,

Time on Earth 6, 7
  Sunrise, Noon, Sunset, Midnight 2, 6
  STANDARD Time (Greenwich Time) 11,
  Equivalent Greenwich Mean Time (EGMT) 11,13
  Local Mean Time (LMT) 10,
  Time Zones in the United States 11,
  SIDEREAL Time 11,
  Daylight Saving Time 14,

The HOUSES 3, 6
  The Cusps and Midpoints 3,44
  Angular, Succeedent & Cadent Houses 3,
  Diurnal & Nocturnal Houses 3,
  Quadrants and Midpoints 3,44

The SIGNS: Name, Symbol, Quality & Element 4, 6
  Equinox & Solstice Signs 7,
  Intercepted Signs 23,27
  Decanates & Faces 34,35

Table of Contents

Subject	Page
The PLANETS	5,
Rulership, Dignity & Debility	5,
Speed of Planets & Time in a Sign	5,37
Planets rising, culminating & setting	6, 7
Longitude of a Planet	16,
Planets Direct, Retrograde & Stationary	18,19
Intercepted Planets	23,27
Planets in Mutual Reception	27,43
Latitude of a Planet	30,
Declination of the Moon	31,
Planets turning in direction	52,
Nodal Points of the Planets	19,62
The TERMS of the Planets	88,
Planetary Rulership of Days & Hours	98,
TO SET UP THE WHEEL	12,
Change Clock Time to Local Mean Time (LMT)	13,
Change Longitude to Time (EGMT)	13,
Finding the Interval since noon	13,
The 10-second Correction	13,
The Sidereal Time, noon previous to birth	14,
The CALCULATED SIDEREAL TIME	14,
For SOUTH Latitude	14,15,24
For EAST Longitude	14,26,28
To use the Table of Houses	15,
Sign & Degree for the Cusps	15,
Correcting the MINUTES for Minor Cusps	15,
Correcting the Angles (M.C. & Ascendant)	32,33
Specimen Work, p.m. West & North	20,21
" " a.m. West & North	22,23
" " p.m. West & South	24,25
" " a.m. East & North	26,27
" " p.m. East & South	28,
" " a.m. East & South	29,

Table of Contents

Subject — Page

Calculating the Planets 16,19
  Longitude of Planets 16,
  The GMT for West Longitude 16,19,20
  The GMT for East Longitude 16,26,29
  The ADDED LINE for the GMT 29,
  The Constant Logarithm (C. Log.) 16,24,26
  Using the Logarithm Card 17,
  Which Planets to Calculate 17,
  Specimen Lines from the Ephemeris 17,
  Equating the Slow Planets 17,21,24
  The Dates to use 18,
  Retrograde Planets 18,19
  Stationary Planets 19,
  Planets changing Signs (Moon & Venus) 19,20
  Equating the Moon's Nodes 19,25
  Entering the Planets in the Houses 21,
  Latitude of Planets 30,
  Declination of Planets 31,83
  " Increasing, Decreasing, Changing 31,
  Midpoints involving Planets 44,
  Moon leaving the Sign 45,
  The Solstice Points of the Planets 85,

Using the Midnight Ephemeris 86,87
  Finding the Interval 86,87
  The Sidereal Time to use 86,
  The Calc. S. T. for South & East 86,
  The GMT and Constant Logarithm 87,
  To add or subtract the small motion 87,

The International Date Line 84,
  The Prime Meridian it contacts 84,
  The EGMT either East or West of 180 84,
  Finding the GMT and Constant Log 84,

Table of Contents

Subject	Page
ASPECTS	36 to 40
Names and symbols	36 to 40
Partile & Platic Aspects	36,
Applying & Separating Aspects	36,37
Less-used Aspects	40,
Parallel of Declination	40,83
The ORB to allow	41,
The Lunation, Eclipse & Occultation	42,43
Listing the Aspects	43,
The aspects allowed the Horary Moon	45,
Using the ASPECTARIAN in the Ephemeris ...	45,
Secondary Progression	46,
The Progressed Date	46,47,49
The Sidereal Time to use	46,47,49
Finding the Increase in Sidereal Time	46,47,49
Finding the Progressed Sidereal Time	46,47,49
The Latitude to use	46,47,49
The Cusps for SOUTH Latitude	46,49
The GMT and Constant Log. to use	46,47,49
The Prog. Moon & her monthly motion	47,
The Month-by-Month Moon & her aspects	48,
Specimen Progressed Chart	49,
Applying the progressed aspects	48,49
Showing the progressions around the wheel.	49,
Progressing for Planets changing direction	52,
RECTIFICATION by Secondary Progression	50,51
Working with the Midheaven	50,
Working with the Ascendant	51,
The Adjusted Calculation Date (A.C.D.)	92,93
The Ephemeris to use	92,93
Finding the Sidereal Time for the A.C.D...	92,93

Table of Contents

Subject	Page
The RADIX System	54,
Advantages of the Radix System	54,
The Solar or MAJOR Arc	54,
Direct Directing	54,
Converse Directing	54,59
TABLE of Major Arcs	55,
The Lunar or MINOR Arc	56,
The Minor Moon	56,
TABLE of Minor Arcs	57,
Rate of Progression and ORB	58,
The Oblique Ascendant, Direct & Converse	58,59
The Oblique Fortuna	58,
The Converse MINOR Moon	59,
MUNDANE Parallels	60,
Meridian Parallel (MP)	60,
Horizontal " (HP)	60,
Rapt " (RP)	60,
Quadrate " (QP)	61,
Directional " (DP)	61,
The JOHNDRO Locality Charts	72,
Right Ascension (R.A.) and diagram	72,
The Planets to use	72,74
CORRECTION TABLE for 46.10"	73,
Right Ascension of the SUN	74,
To find the R.A. of the Midheaven	74,75
Specimen BIRTH Locality Chart	75,79
A Personal Locality Chart	76,77
Directing on a Placidian Arc	77,
A WORLD Chart (for Tel Aviv)	78,79
Solar HOUSES	63,
The Sign on the Ascendant	63,
The Planets to use	63,

Table of Contents

Subject	Page
The INGRESS Charts	80,
The Four Ingresses	80,
Finding the Log/Distance	80,81
Finding the Log/Motion	80,81
Finding the Log/Time	80,81
Finding the GMT/Interval & Constant Log	80,81
Finding the LMT	80,81
Working the LONDON Ingress Chart	81,
Working the Ingress for other localities	82,
The Planets to use	82,
Specimen Ingress Chart, Autumnal Equinox	83,
The SOLAR Return (Revolution)	66,
The Ephemeris to use	66,
The Birth Data required	66,67
Finding the S.T. for the Solar Return	66,67
The LATITUDE to use	66,
Finding & marking the Solar LMT	66,67
Finding the Solar GMT	66,115
Finding the Solar Constant Log	66,67
The Planets to calculate	66,67
The ORB to allow	66,
Specimen Solar Return Chart	67,
Solar Return TABLE for Age-Equivalent	68,
Reading the Solar Return Chart	69,
The LUNAR Return	70,71
The Permanent TABLE (Personal)	70,
The Lunar Constant	71,115
Finding the Minor Moon	71,116
Specimen natal chart with Lunar Return	71,
The TERMS of the Planets	88,
The Egyptian TABLE of Terms	88,

Table of Contents vii

Subject	Page
The DIURNAL Chart	89,90
The Ephemeris to use	89,90
The Time, Place & Constant Log. to use	89,
Finding the significant lunation & date	89,90
Calculating the Moon	90,
Specimen Diurnal Chart & delineation	91,
The LIFE CYCLE Chart	96,
The Ascendant and other cusps	96,97
The Quadrants, Houses & Sections	96,
Specimen Life Cycle Chart & Events	97,
The Present-Age Planet	64,
TABLE I for the Planets	64,
TABLE II for the Ages	64,
Specimen Chart and Delineation	65,
Prominent DEGREES	53,
The Critical Degrees	53,37,48
Malefic Fixed-Star Degrees	53,
Benefic Fixed-Star Degrees	53,75
The Arabian Points (PARTS)	94,95
The Part of Fortune	22,26
" " " Marriage (M)	94,
" " " Deaths (D)	94,
" " " Sickness (S)	95,
" " " Peril (P)	95,
" " " Legacies (L)	95,
Questions & Answers	101-125

****

FOREWORD

This work is designed for use as a textbook in setting up a chart for the exact location of the planets for any given date, hour and place on earth. It also goes further, to include progressing the chart to show the advanced positions at any desired future date.

Because many students are not conveniently close to a school of astrology, and also because many want this type of specialized reference long after they have completed their mathematical training, this work is so arranged that it can be learned entirely at home and may be referred to throughout the following years when the mathematical need may arise.

At the end of each lesson, the pupil should turn to the examination questions covering that lesson, at the back of the book, and try to give the answers, so that any point not sufficiently clear may be gone over once more. Repetition at this time will establish the principles at the outset and in their proper order, making the way clear for the next step.

The student will need an Ephemeris (a booklet which is issued for each year, giving the Sidereal Time and the planet places for each day): a logarithm card saving much calculating: a Table of Houses (list of Signs on cusps) and a pierced template for drawing the wheel as on page 2 herein. It is desirable to also possess Dernay's LONGITUDES AND LATITUDES IN THE UNITED STATES and his LONGITUDES AND LATITUDES THROUGHOUT THE WORLD, which include the Difference in Time, and the Equivalent Greenwich Mean Time already figured for the pupil.

FOUNDATION OF THE ASTROLOGICAL CHART

Our Solar System

The vast reaches of Space surrounding our Earth form what is called the Celestial Sphere, through which are scattered 88 Constellations (groups of fixed stars) of which 56 are within the Equatorial Zone, which extends from 45 degrees above the equator to 45 degrees below: 23 are within 45 degrees of the South Pole, and only 9 within 45 degrees of the North Pole.

Of the 88, twelve in the Equatorial Zone form the 360 degree circle of the Zodiac, and fall irregularly near the twelve 30-degree sections called SIGNS & originally identified with them but no longer in the same places. It is not the constellations that we use but these 30-degree Signs, which are precise mathematical divisions always in the same position in the great circle.

Besides the fixed stars in the constellations, there is the SUN, the one great fixed star marking the point around which the non-fixed celestial bodies revolve, & so becoming the center of our Solar System. It is the Sun which is the basis of our calculations, giving what is called Sidereal (star) Time if we are figuring from his path, the zodiac or ECLIPTIC: and Right Ascension, if we are figuring from his relationship to the Celestial Equator, as we shall see later in this work.

The Moon is our Earth's satellite, neither a star nor a planet but of immense importance as the prime activator in our affairs, being closest to us. Then we have the eight planets or "wandering stars" each in its own orbit or path around the Sun. These also differ from the Sun and Moon in that they sometimes appear to move in a backward or RETROGRADE direction. (See page 18.)

FOUNDATION OF THE ASTROLOGICAL CHART

The Basic Wheel

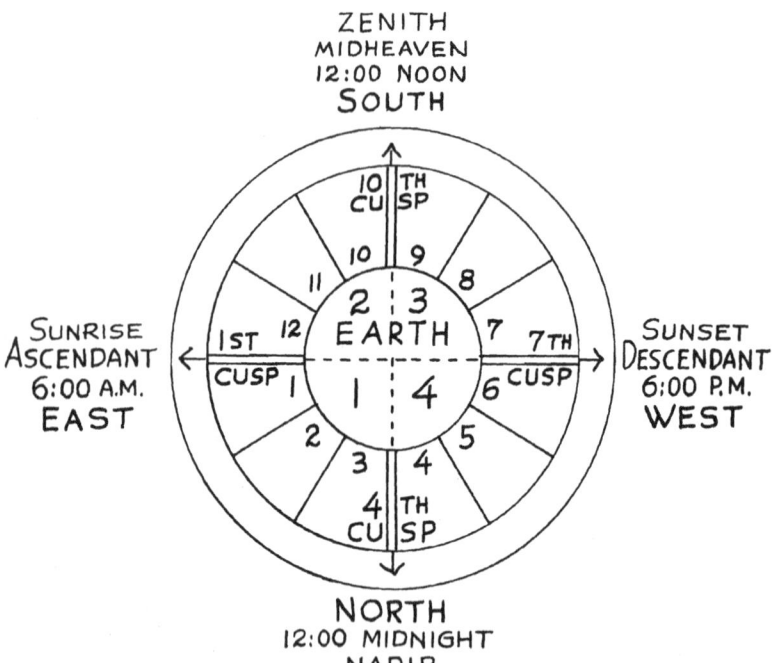

The Direction Angles of the Chart are the 1st cusp (indicating Sunrise, therefore the Eastern HORIZON), the 10th cusp (denoting Noon therefore the South MERIDIAN), the 7th cusp (indicating Sunset, therefore the Western HORIZON), and the 4th cusp (denoting Midnight, therefore the North MERIDIAN). These are based on the Sun's relationship to the equator at noon and in the Northern Hemisphere where we look south to see him at his zenith.

The HOUSES

In the center of the wheel on page 2 is the circle of the Earth, divided into four quadrants by dotted lines which mark the equator and meridian. Around this is a large circle representing conditions on the surface of the Earth and divided into 12 parts. Beyond this, the outer circle marks the outer limits of our solar system and is a broad band containing the twelve Signs of the Zodiac through the center of which runs the 360-degree path of the Sun which we call the Ecliptic.

Conditions on the face of the Earth form what we call the WORLD & its affairs, which we allot to departments called Houses. There are 12 of these, theoretically containing 30 degrees each to correspond with the Signs but some contain more and some less because of what is called "the obliquity of the ecliptic" or deviation of the Sun's path from paralleling the Celestial Equator, which is the Earth's equator projected out into space.

The Cusp is the divisional line marking the beginning of the House. The Ascendant is the cusp of the First House; the next line lower marks the cusp of the Second House, and so on around the wheel. Houses 1 to 6 inclusive are below the horizon in the nocturnal (night) half of the chart. Houses 7 to 12 are in the diurnal (day) half of the chart.

The 1st, 4th, 7th and 10th are the ANGULAR houses of the wheel. Each one is followed by a SUCCEEDENT house (the 2nd, 5th, 8th and 11th) which in turn is followed by a CADENT house (the 3rd, 6th, 9th and 12th). Planets in these houses operate with more publicity by being angular, less publicity by being succeedent, still less by being cadent (although the Sun throws light on the best of any house he is in at birth). Each quadrant contains an angular, succeedent and cadent house.

FOUNDATION OF THE ASTROLOGICAL CHART

The 12 Signs

The great circle outlining the limits of space as we look out from our place on Earth is like any other circle, large or small, in that it contains 360 degrees. It is an entirely mathematical entity, divided into 12 mathematical sections of 30 degrees each which we call Signs, whose names, symbols & numbers are as follows:

No.	Name	Symbol		No.	Name	Symbol
1st	Aries	♈	opposite	7th	Libra	♎
2nd	Taurus	♉	"	8th	Scorpio	♏
3rd	Gemini	♊	"	9th	Sagittarius	♐
4th	Cancer	♋	"	10th	Capricorn	♑
5th	Leo	♌	"	11th	Aquarius	♒
6th	Virgo	♍	"	12th	Pisces	♓

The odd-numbered Signs are masculine & positive (radiating out). The even-numbered Signs are feminine & negative (attracting within). By Quality (Cardinal, Fixed & Common or Mutable) and by Element (Fire, Earth, Air and Water) the Signs are as follows:

	Fire	Earth	Air	Water
Cardinal	Aries	Capri	Libra	Cancer
Fixed	Leo	Taurus	Aquar	Scorpio
Common	Sagit	Virgo	Gemini	Pisces

Cardinal Signs inaugurate, Fixed Signs establish, Common Signs adapt to existing circumstances. Fire Signs are spiritual, Earth Signs practical, Air Signs intellectual, and Water Signs emotional.

The Sun, Moon and 8 Planets

Against the backdrop or curtain of the 12 Signs, The Sun, Moon and planets are seen to move, and are therefore said to be "in" those Signs. They have certain standing in certain Signs more than others, so that we say each celestial body "rules" a particular Sign & is "dignified" there; "detrimented" in the opposite Sign, "exalted" in another Sign and "in its fall" in the opposite one, as follows:

Planet	Dignity	Detriment	Exaltation	In Fall
The Sun	Leo	Aquar	Aries	Libra
" Moon	Cancer	Capri	Taurus	Scorpio
Mercury	Gem/Vir	Sagit	Virgo	Pisces
Venus	Tau/Lib	Ari/Scorp	Pisces	Virgo
Mars	Ari/Scorp	Lib/Tau	Capri	Cancer
Jupiter	Sagit	Gemini	Cancer	Capri
Saturn	Capri	Cancer	Libra	Aries
Uranus	Aquar	Leo	Scorpio	Taurus
Neptune	Pisces	Virgo	Gemini	Sagit
Pluto	Scorpio	Taurus	?	?

Planetary Motion

Symbol		Daily Motion	In a Sign
☿	Moon	13:11:00	2½ days
☽	Mercury	1:23:00	variable days
♀	Venus	1:12:00	variable month
☉	Sun	0:59:08	1 month
♂	Mars	0:33:28	variable month
♃	Jupiter	0:04:59	1 year
♄	Saturn	0:02:00	2½ years
♅	Uranus	0:00:42	7 years
♆	Neptune	0:00:22	14 years
♇	Pluto	0:00:13	23/25 years

6   FOUNDATION OF THE ASTROLOGICAL CHART

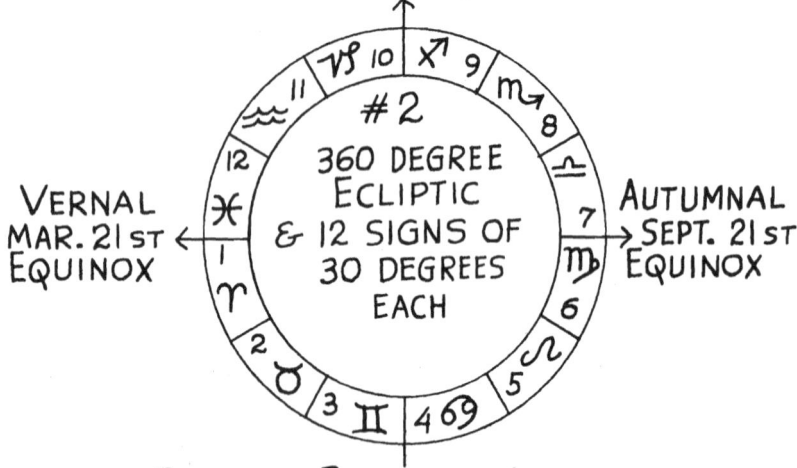

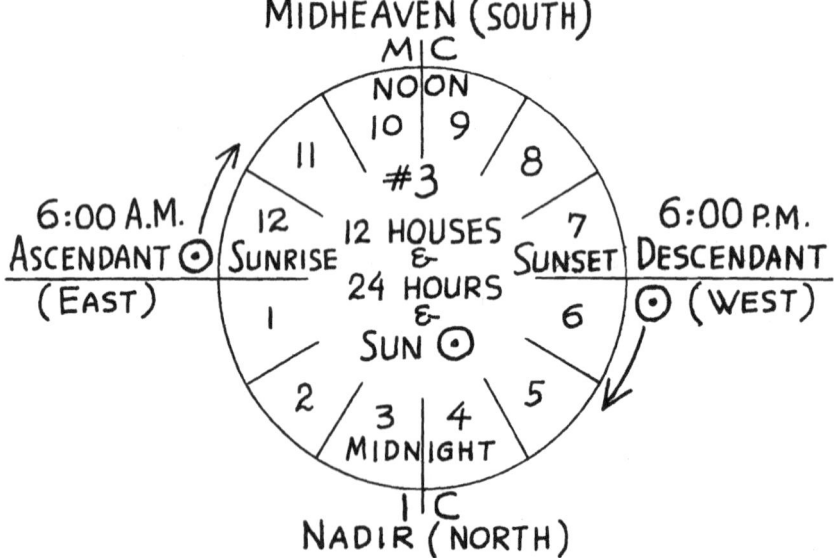

The CHART

The chart is made up of two wheels which combine the heavens above by Signs as shown by Chart #2 on page 6, with the earth below by clock time and departments of human activity called Houses, as shown by Chart #3.

The astrological year begins on March 21st, when the Sun enters 0-Aries, the beginning of Spring, the time of the Vernal Equinox when his path crosses the Celestial Equator and days and nights are of equal length. This happens again on September 21st when he enters 0-Libra at the Autumnal Equinox. When he is farthest from the Celestial Equator he marks the Summer Solstice on June 21st and the Winter Solstice on December 21st, when he apparently stands still (sol-stice) while turning back from 0-Cancer & 0-Capricorn to the Celestial Equator.

The Sun tells the time

It is the Sun by House that tells the time for which the chart was set: he "establishes" the chart. Note that Chart #3 shows that the Sun rises at 6:00 a.m. on the Ascend-ant or 1st cusp, moving to the Midheaven at noon and falling to the Descendant at sunset. The even hour falls on the cusp, the uneven hour in the middle of the House. For Chart #3, the Sun will conjunct the 12th cusp at 8:00 a.m., and by 9:00 a.m. he will be in the middle of the 11th House.

The motion of the planets in the wheel

Planets RISE when they reach and leave the 1st cusp. They CULMINATE at the 10th cusp and SET at the 7th, and are lowest at the 4th cusp, after which they begin to rise again. This is because the Earth turns counter-clockwise, taking the Houses DOWN with it so that cusps seem to pass the planets, making them appear to go UP.

FOUNDATION OF THE ASTROLOGICAL CHART

The Parallels of Latitude

The Chinese say that one picture is worth a thousand words. To save that many, let us look at the diagram below, picturing a hemisphere, or the southern half of the sphere on which we live.

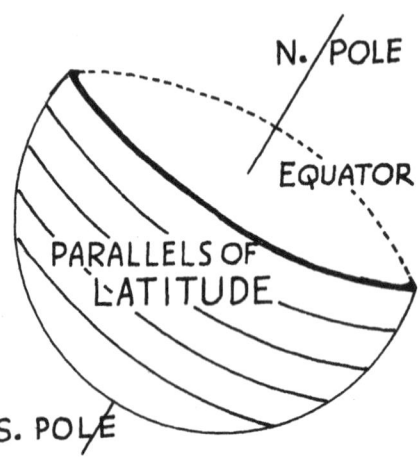

Parallel lines are those that maintain the same distance apart and never meet each other. The great circle of the Equator divides the whole sphere into North and South halves, each of which measures her 90-degree distance to the North or South Pole. This distance is marked off by parallel lines of LATITUDE and there are 90 of them north of the Equator & 90 south, all circles like herself, each measuring 360 degrees and returning to itself. The Equator lies in the Torrid Zone halfway between the Tropic of Cancer & the Tropic of Capricorn each of which is 23-deg 27-min distant from her, which is to say 23:27 North Latitude & 23:27 South Latitude.

Geographical Longitude

   This diagram also pictures a hemisphere, the western half of the sphere on which we live. The only earthly straight line is that which connects the North & South Poles - because it runs straight through the center of the globe and ends abruptly without further reference. All the others are "laid" on the curved outer surface, making all other lines great circles.

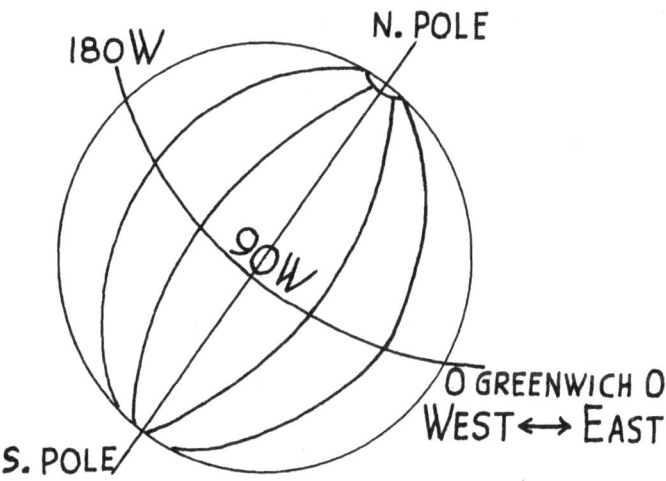

   The great circles connecting the Poles and continuing on the other side of the globe, returning to themselves and each other at the Poles, are MERIDIANS marking distance east and west of 0-degrees. They are one degree apart and there are 360 of them, 180 being East and 180 West of the starting point at Greenwich. Longitude is distance East and West of Meridian 0-degrees.

   Any locality will be on one of these meridians and at the same time on one of the parallels of latitude. We say "Cross marks the spot" meaning the cross formed by the N-to-S Longitude line & the E-to-W Latitude line.

The PRIME Meridians

The word meridian means "noon", and all geographical places on a meridian, no matter how far north or south of the equator, have noon at the same instant, because both poles connected by the meridian are presented simultaneously to the Sun who brings NOON down the line.

Of the 360 meridians, 24 are called Prime Meridians. These are 15 degrees apart, starting at a point designated 0, which is located at the Greenwich Observatory in England where Standard Time is reckoned and planetary places calculated.

The 24 Prime Meridians mark the arrival of the noontime Sun every hour on the hour as it were, around the earth, starting at noon at 0-degrees Greenwich & marking the noon hour somewhere in regular order each hour of the 24 thereafter.

Every 15 degrees of longitude (or whole distance between Prime Meridians) equals 1 hour of time or 60 minutes. (One degree therefore equals 4 minutes of time.) Localities that are 15 degrees apart in distance are 1 hour apart in time, the Sun requiring that much time to travel that far between them. (In reality, the Earth turns and presents the Meridians to the fixed Sun.)

Every locality BETWEEN Prime Meridians marks its own north-to-south line called its Local Meridian which is the basis of its longitude or distance from Greenwich. We find this in an atlas or map or, as advised in the Foreword, by using Dernay's books, which give this and other calculations already figured for us.

The Prime Meridians, cont'd

Since it takes the Sun 24 hours to circle the globe, we accordingly have 24 Prime Meridians, 12 of them being east of Greenwich and 12 west. They are numbered in Degrees as follows and their corresponding distance from Greenwich is also stated beneath them in Hours:

The Prime Meridians

EAST of Greenwich

0	15	30	45	60	75	90	105	120	135	150	165	180
0	1	2	3	4	5	6	7	8	9	10	11	12

180	165	150	135	120	105	90	75	60	45	30	15	0
12	11	10	9	8	7	6	5	4	3	2	1	0

WEST of Greenwich

Prime Meridian 0 designates STANDARD TIME which is set in Greenwich for the world. Noon arrives there while it is 4:00 a.m. at 120 West Longitude (8 hours away) & 8:00 p.m. at 120 East Longitude (8 hours away also but time east of Greenwich is later than Greenwich Time).

The 4 Prime Meridians in the United States

```
75W  = Eastern Standard Time (EST)
90W  = Central    "       "  (CST)
105W = Mountain   "       "  (MST)
120W = Pacific    "       "  (PST)
```

All clocks between Prime Meridians are set to show the time at their nearest Prime Meridian -- not the actual time at their own locality. We call this "Clock Time" and make a correction accordingly in these time zones to LOCAL Mean Time for exactitude. In the ephemeris, the Sun's daily position is given by Sign-and-degree & by its equivalent in Sidereal Time which is 10 seconds faster than Clock Time.   (See Step #5 on page 13.)

FOUNDATION OF THE ASTROLOGICAL CHART

To Set Up a Chart

1. RELATE THE BIRTHPLACE TO ITS NEAREST PRIME MERIDIAN (mark it plus on the right side, minus on the left)

   Native born in New York City. The map gives this location on LOCAL Meridian 74W. The nearest Prime Meridian is 75 West, a difference of 1 degree EAST (on the plus side) of 75 West or 4 minutes to plus.

2. CHANGE THE CLOCK TIME TO LOCAL MEAN TIME (the LMT).

   a - When birthplace is EAST of the Prime Meridian PLUS 4 minutes for each degree of difference.
   b - When birthplace is WEST of the Prime Meridian MINUS 4 minutes for each degree of difference.

   Examples:

   c - 5:50 a.m. is what time at 69 West? It is on the PLUS side of Prime Meridian 75 W, a difference of 6 degrees or (6 x 4) 24 minutes to PLUS.

   ```
   5:50 a.m. Clock Time
   + :24 Difference east of 75 W
   5:74 (reduce 74 min. to 1:14)
   6:14 a.m. LOCAL Mean Time
   ```

   d - 4:20 p.m. is what time at 69 East? It is on the MINUS side of Prime Meridian 75 E, a difference of 6 degrees or (6 x 4) minutes to MINUS.

   ```
   4:20 p.m. Clock Time
   - :24 Difference west of 75 E
   3:56 p.m. LOCAL Mean Time
   ```

To Set Up a Chart, cont'd   13

3. FIND THE INTERVAL (the time elapsed between the LMT
   and its preceding noon). A p.m. Local Mean Time is
   the time elapsed since noon; mark it INTERVAL. But
   an a.m. Local Mean Time is since midnight & we have
   to add 12 hours to find the interval since noon:

   e -   6:14:00 a.m. LMT (since midnight)
            + 12:00:00 midnight to previous noon
               18:14:00 the INTERVAL (since noon)

4. CHANGE DISTANCE (Longitude) TO TIME. Call the result "Equivalent Greenwich Mean Time", or the EGMT.

   Rule: Multiply the longitude by 4 minutes (the number of minutes in 1 degree) & divide by 60 minutes.

   f -   117 degrees of longitude
            x 4 minutes in 1 degree
         60'/468 minutes /7 hours 48 minutes = 7:48 EGMT
            420
             48 minutes

5. FIND 10-second CORRECTION FOR BOTH EGMT & INTERVAL.
   (Sidereal Time & Clock Time differ to this extent.)

   Instead of multiplying the hours & minutes separately by 1∅ seconds & dividing by 6∅ seconds, discard
   the final zero in each figure & simply divide by 6.
   Set down the seconds-dots; divide the HOURS by 6, &
   set down on left of dots with remainder on right of
   dots, leaving a space. Divide the MINUTES by 6 and
   set down in remaining space. Disregard any SECONDS.

   g - 7:48:22 EGMT   h - 18:14:09 INTERVAL
        1:18 Correction   3:02 Correction

6. FIND THE SIDEREAL TIME, NOON PREVIOUS TO BIRTH, IN THE EPHEMERIS. Take the Ephemeris issued for the year of birth and turn to the page for the month of birth, noting there the column headed Sidereal Time.

   i - If the birth hour is a.m., the noon previous to birth will be for the day BEFORE the birthdate.
   j - If the birth hour is p.m., the noon previous to birth will be for the same day as the birthdate.

7. COMBINE THE FOREGOING FINDINGS under the heading of Hour, Minute, Second. (See specimen work, page 20.)

   k - The birth hour *(corrected from Daylight Saving Time if necessary) marked a.m. or p.m. & dated.
   l - Add or subtract difference from Prime Meridian as in c and d, and mark it LMT, a.m. or p.m.
   m - Add 12:00:00 hours if a.m. LMT (not otherwise). The total shown by l or m is to be marked INT.
   n - Add the 10-second correction for the Interval.
   o - Add 10-second correction for the EGMT if birthplace is in West Longitude (but not otherwise).
   p - Add Sidereal Time (according to i and j above).
   q - Add 12:00:00 hours if birthplace is South Latitude, but not otherwise.
   r - If the sum of these exceeds 24:00:00 (one whole sidereal day having passed) deduct 24:00:00 hrs.
   s - Subtract the 10-second correction for the EGMT if the birthplace is in East Longitude.
   t - Mark the result the CALCULATED SIDEREAL TIME.

* The Daylight Saving Time period differs throughout the world, both as to date of beginning and ending and as to advancing the clock by one or more hours - which must be corrected for your use under k above. It is advisable to own Curran & Taylor's "WORLD D. S. TIME".

The Sign-&-Degree for the Cusps

Example

Using Dalton's Table of Houses page 3, find Sidereal Time nearest 00:23:01 Calculated Sidereal Time. It is at the top of the page heading the first column on the left side of the page, and is 0:22:02. This points to 6 Aries for the Midheaven for any chart, any Latitude.

For NORTH Latitude

If the birthplace is in North Latitude, say 26, this 6 Aries goes on the 10th cusp, and 15:50 Cancer is put on the 1st cusp because it is under the heading 1 and on line 26 under the heading Lat. These two, the Midheaven and Ascendant, are taken just as they are given.

The MINUTES of the remaining cusps are in tenths and are to be multiplied by 6. Thus, the 11th (given as Taurus 10.4) is set down in the chart as Taurus 10:24. The 12th will be Gemini 14:36; the 2nd, Leo 9:06 & the 3rd, Virgo 5:18. Their opposite cusps will have the same degree-&-minute but the opposite Sign.

For SOUTH Latitude

If the birthplace is in South Latitude 26, however, you would have added 12:00:00 in finding the Calculated Sidereal Time which would then be 12:23:01 pointing to 6 Libra (see Dalton's Table, page 35). This is placed on the 4th cusp, not the 10th; the 5th is next instead of the 11th and so on, remembering to correct the minutes: the 5th will be Scorpio 5:36 (not 5.6); the 6th, Sagittarius 0:42; the Descendant Sagittarius 23:55 because it is not in tenths. (See the work on page 24.)

Calculation of the Planets

The longitude of a planet is its distance in a Sign its degree and minute. These places are given in the ephemeris for noon each day and for Greenwich. Anyone born there & then would find the places made to order, requiring no calculation. A birth occurring at a different time & place, however, demands a certain simple mathematical adjustment, for which we need a "constant logarithm" representing the native's birthplace & time taken back to Greenwich, so to speak.

The Greenwich Mean Time (GMT)
& Constant Logarithm (C. Log)

RULE

The LMT plus the EGMT equals the GMT
for births in West Longitude.
The LMT minus the EGMT equals the GMT
for births in East Longitude.
Mark the GMT a.m. or p.m. & date it.
(This is the GMT-line.)
A p.m. GMT is changed at once to the
C. Log (use the logarithm card).
An a.m. GMT is subtracted from noon
(call it 11:60) and the result is
changed to the C. Log.

```
  10:15 a.m. LMT June 2nd        10:15 p.m. LMT June 2nd
+  7:53 EGMT W. Longitude      +  7:53 EGMT W. Longitude
  18:08 past a.m.                 18:08 past p.m.
- 12:00 noon today              -12:00 midnight tonight
   6:08 p.m. GMT June 2nd         6:08 a.m. GMT June 3rd
        CHANGE AT ONCE      from 11:60 SUBTRACT & CHANGE
  6:08 p.m. = .5925 C. Log.       5:52 = .6118 C. Log.
```

Calculation of the Planets

The Logarithm Card

The logarithm card is the same as the Table of Logarithms on the last page of the ephemeris, but the print is larger and clearer: figures are not easily mistaken for others. Using the foregoing example, 6:08 GMT, we find the 6 hours along the top of the Table, and the 8 minutes down the side column: the figure to which they both lead in the body of the Table is 5925 the C. Log. Write it down and underscore it for ready finding.

Always calculate the exact places for the Sun, Moon, and three faster planets Mercury, Venus and Mars.

Specimen lines from Raphael's Ephemeris
September, 1936

Da Mo	Sidereal Time	☉ Long.	☽ Long.	♂ Long.	♀ Long.	☿ Long.
27			17 Aq 45			℞
28	12:28:20	5 Li 10	2 Pi 01	1 Vi 11	29 Li 40	10 Li 28
29	12:32:16	6 " 9	16 " 44	1 " 48	00 Sc 54	9 " 22

The slow-moving planets Jupiter, Saturn, Uranus, Neptune and Pluto are easily calculated mentally. When the LMT & GMT are both the same date, the slow planets are used as given on that date because they have moved too little to calculate. But if the LMT is p.m. & the GMT a.m. so that midnight comes between them involving two dates, divide their small difference in motion between them by simple mental equation. Jupiter on Sept. 28th in Sagittarius 17:56 moves 8 minutes to Sagittarius 18:04 on Sept. 29th so we allow half the difference in motion or 4 minutes per day, giving Jupiter's place as 18:00 Sagittarius.

FOUNDATION OF THE ASTROLOGICAL CHART

The dates to use

The GMT-line tells you. Always start with the date on the GMT-line, so be sure to put it there: we are to use it twice in working the planets. See Moon, p. 19.

RULE: P.m. means plus: A.m. means minus. For a p.m. GMT, take the planet on the GMT-date and a date plus, (the following day). For an a.m. GMT, take the planet on the GMT-date and a date minus, (the preceding day).

Subtract the planet's place on one day from its place the following day to find its large motion, which will be in hours & minutes. Use the logarithm card to turn this into a logarithm, to which add the Constant Log., which will result in another log. Find the nearest to this in the body of the logarithm card, which will indicate (by pointing UP to the hour-line, and ACROSS to the minute-line) the number of hours-and-minutes representing the small motion, which we are to use.

For a p.m. GMT, plus the small motion to the planetary place on the GMT-date. For an a.m. GMT, minus the small motion from the planetary place on the GMT-date.

Retrograde Planets

When a planet (never the Sun or Moon) is marked "R" it signifies that the planet is seemingly moving backward, due to the earth's passing it & apparently leaving it behind. In this case, we still take the planet as indicated by the GMT-line but subtract upside down, to find the large motion; and we REVERSE the plus-and-minus rule for the small motion. If the GMT-line says to add, we minus; if it says to minus, we add. Compare the Direct and Retrograde examples on page 19.

Calculation of the Planets

Specimen Work

The GMT & Constant Log.

1:15 a.m. LMT Sept 28
+ 7:53 EGMT West Longit
9:08 a.m. GMT Sept 28
(subtract)
11:60
2:52 = .9928 the C.L.

The Moon

28th *2:01 Pisces
27th -17:45 Aquarius
  14:16 = 2259 log.
     + 9928 C.L.
28th - 1:27 = 12187 log.
  0:34 Pisces

*In subtracting the Moon's place in Aquarius 17:45 from the lesser figure, 2:01 Pisces, add 30 degrees to make it 32:01 Pisces, calling it 31:61 in order to subtract.

A planet as though Direct and as though Retrograde

Direct
28th 11:32 Libra
27th 10:28 Libra
  1:04 = 13522 log.
    + 9928 C.L.
28th -0:07 = 23450 log.
 11:25 Libra

Retrograde
28th -10:28 Libra
27th 11:32 Libra
  1:04 = 13522 log.
    + 9928 C.L.
28th + 0:07 = 23450 log.
 10:35 R Libra

The letter "S" signifies STATIONARY: the planet is between Direct and Retrograde, requiring no calculation.

The North & South NODES of the Moon are points related to her contact in crossing the ecliptic into North and South Latitude. At the top of the right-hand page of Raphael's Ephemeris we see the N. Node given for every other day & always retrograde at the rate of 3 minutes per day. See Chart #6, page 25, and the text below.

FOUNDATION OF THE ASTROLOGICAL CHART

Work for P.M. Chart W-Longit & N-Lat

1:08:00 p.m. PST Sept. 28, 1936, 118W15 34N

```
 1:08:00 pm PST Sept. 28                    Cusps
∱  7:00   Diff. E of 120W
 1:15:00 pm LMT-Interval              (10th .. 28:00 Libra
 0:12    correction Int.              (11th .. 24.0  Scorp
 1:18  "  EGMT 7:53:00                (12th .. 16.2  Sagit
∱12:28:20 Sid. Time, 28th             ( 1st .. 8:28  Capri
 13:44:50 Calculated S.T.             ( 2nd .. 16.1  Aquar
 13:44:00 Nearest in Table ... 34N    ( 3rd .. 25.2  Pisces
```

GMT and Constant Log.   **Moon**

```
                                    29th  16:44 Pisces
 1:15 pm LMT Sept 28                28th - 2:01 Pisces
∱ 7:53 EGMT W. Longit                     14:53 = 2124 log.
 9:08 pm GMT Sept 28                            ∱ 4196 C.L.
                                    28th ∱ 5:36 = 6320 log.
 .4196 Constant Log.                      7:37 Pisces
```

```
          Sun          Merc R         Mars           Venus
29th    6:09 Li      -9:22 Li       1:48 Vi       00:54 Scorpio
28th   -5:10 Li      10:28 Li       1:11 Vi       29:40 Libra
        0:59          1:06          0:37           1:14 = 12891
     = 13875         13388         15902                ∱ 4196
     ∱  4196          4196          4196          ∱ 0:28 = 17087
        18071        17584         20098          29:68 (Reduce
28th ∱0:22          -0:26         ∱0:14           ∱1-60
        5:32 Li    R 10:02 Li      1:25 Vi        00:08 Scorpio
```

Note quick method of setting down Sun, Mercury & Mars.
Note Venus: 0:28 added to 29:40 Libra takes her out of
Libra and into Scorpio. (68 minutes reduces to 1:08.)

P.M. Chart, West Longitude & North Latitude   21

1:08:00 pm PST Sept 28 1936   12:28:20 Sid. Time, 28th
9:08 pm GMT 28th = .4196 CL   13:44:50 Calc. Sid. Time

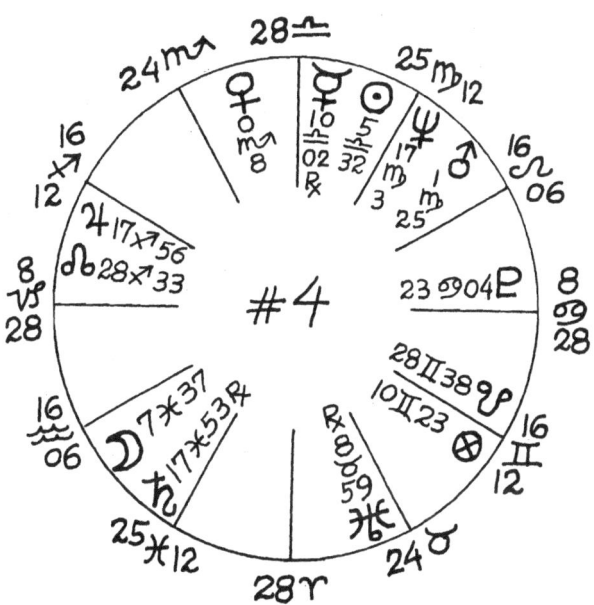

Note that the Signs move counter-clockwise. Capricorn the 10th Sign on the 1st cusp moves downward toward the 11th Sign Aquarius. A planet in a house is placed according to its degree in relationship to the degree on the cusp carrying the same Sign. Note the 6th cusp in 16 Gemini, which is between Fortuna in 10 Gemini & the South Node in 28 Gemini: Fortuna is moving TO THE CUSP and the South Node is moving AWAY FROM THE CUSP, which tells us which houses they are to be in.

The LMT & GMT have the same date (page 17) so that the slow planets have hardly moved: do not calculate them.

FOUNDATION OF THE ASTROLOGICAL CHART

Work for A.M. chart W-Longit & N-Lat

1:08:00 a.m. PST Sept. 28, 1936, 118W15 34N

```
  1:08:00 a.m. PST Sept 28              1:15 am LMT Sept 28
/ 7:00    Diff. E of 120W             / 7:53 EGMT W. Longit
  1:15:00 a.m. LMT (not Int           - 9:08 am GMT Sept 28
/12:00:00 to previous noon              11:60
 13:15:00 the Interval                   2:52 = 9928 C. Log.
  2:12 correction Int.
  1:18 "    EGMT 7:53:00              (10th .. 28:00 Aries
/12:24:23 Sid. Time, 27th             (11th ..  3.1 Gemini
 25:42:53 more than 24 hrs            (12th ..  6.5 Cancer
-24:00:00 one sidereal day            ( 1st ..  6:44 L e o
  1:42:53 CALCULATED S. T.            ( 2nd .. 29.3  L e o
  1:44:00 Nearest in Table .. 34N    ( 3rd .. 26.1  Virgo
```

```
          Sun         Merc R       Venus         Moon
28th    5:10 Li     -10:28 Li    29:40 Li    2:01 Pi. or 32:01
27th   -4:11 Li      11:32 Li    28:27 Li   17:45 Aquarius
        0:59          1:04        1:13      14:16 =   2259 log.
     = 13875         13522       12950           /  9928 C.L.
     /  9928          9928        9928      -1:27 = 12187 log.
       23803         23450       22178       0:34 Pisces
28th   -0:06         /0:07       -0:09
        5:04 Li    R10:35 Li    29:31 Li
```

⊗ The Part of Fortune (Fortuna)

```
             S. dg mn
Ascend.    4 06:44      Ascendant plus Moon & then minus Sun
/ Moon    11 00:34      gives Fortuna. Moon has not complet-
       = 15 07:18       ed the 12th Sign: she is 11 Signs &
- Sun     6 05:04       00:34 more. (The ANSWER is Capricorn
         (9) 2:14       because Fortuna finished 9 Signs and
Capricorn    2:14       is 2:14 into the 10th, Capricorn.)
```

A.M. Chart, West Longitude & North Latitude   23

1:08:00 am PST Sept 28 1936   12:24:23 Sid. Time, 27th
9:08 am GMT 28th = .9928 CL   1:42:53 Calc. Sid. Time

#5

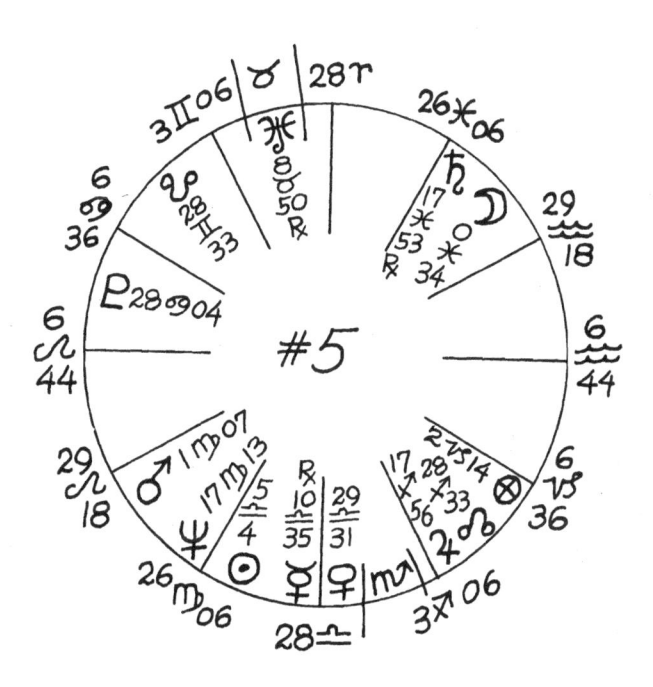

Intercepted Signs and Planets

Note that when the same Sign appears on two cusps (Leo on the 1st & 2nd here, with the opposite Sign Aquarius on the opposite cusps) there will be another Sign that is missing. Here, Aries on the 10th and Gemini on the 11th show that the missing Sign Taurus is between them squeezed into the 10th House: the enclosing lines show that it is INTERCEPTED & so must be the opposite Sign, Scorpio.   Any planet in such a Sign (as Uranus here) is said to be intercepted in that House.

FOUNDATION OF THE ASTROLOGICAL CHART

Work for P.M. Chart, W-Long. & S-Lat

8:35:00 p.m. AST Jan. 22d, 1939, 43W15 23-S

```
  8:35:00 pm AST Jan 22nd  .....  Atlantic Standard Time
+ 7:00    Diff. E of 45 W          Rio de Janeiro, Brazil
  8:42:00 pm LMT Jan 22nd
  1:27    correction Int.
  0:28   "    EGMT 2:53:00
 20:03:46 Sid. Time, 22nd           (4th .. 13:00 Sagit
+12:00:00 for S. Latitude           (5th ..  7.4  Capri
 40:47:41 more than 24 hrs          (6th ..  3.5  Aquar
-24:00:00 one sidereal day          (7th ..  5:44 Pisces
 16:47:41 Calculated S. T.          (8th .. 14.3  Aries
 16:46:16 Nearest in Table ... 23S  (9th .. 16.5  Taurus
```

GMT and Constant Log.	MOON
	23d 4:33 Pisces
8:42 pm LMT Jan 22d	22d -22:38 Aquar.
+ 2:53 EGMT W. Longit	11:55 = 3041 log.
11:35 pm GMT Jan 22d	+ 3164 C.L.
	22d + 5:45 = 6205 log.
.3164 Constant Log.	28:23 Aquarius

By comparison with the P.M. work for Chart #4 page 21, it will be seen that the only difference lies in adding 12:00:00 for South Latitude taking us to the other end of the Meridian, the 4th cusp, where we begin to enter the Signs-&-Degrees, continuing by way of the 5th.

The LMT and GMT are the same date, so the slow planets are taken exactly as given in the ephemeris. We mark Uranus D in the chart because he turned Direct on this very day, signifying that the person whose chart it is will reveal more Uranian traits than otherwise.

P.M. Chart, West Longitude & South Latitude   25

8:35:00 pm AST Jan. 22 1939   20:03:46 Sid. Time, 22nd
11:35 pm GMT 22nd = .3164 CL 16:47:41 Calc. Sid. Time

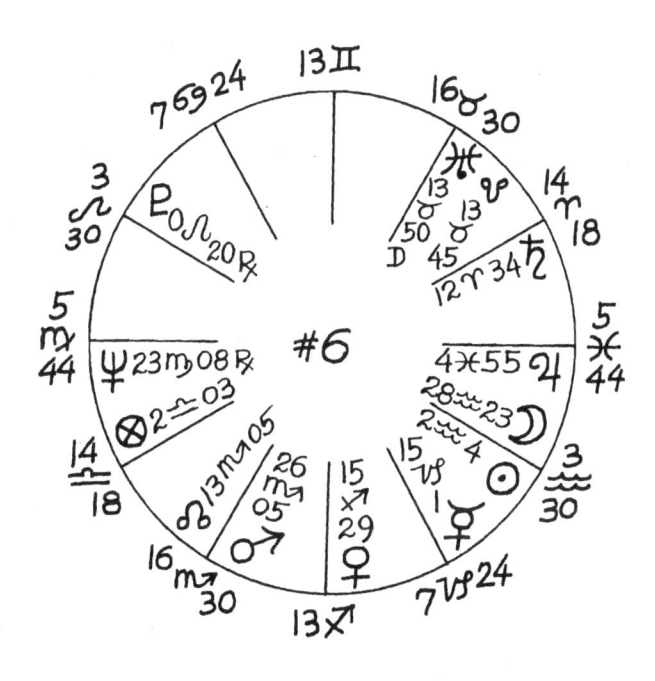

[Astrological chart #6 with the following placements:]

- 13 ♊ (MC)
- 7 ♋ 24, 6 ♋ 9
- 3 ♌ 30
- ♇ 0 ♌ 20 ℞
- 16 ♉ 30
- 13 ♈ ♅ / 13 ♈ ♂ 50 / 45 ☽ D / 12 ♈ 34 ♄
- 14 ♈ 18
- 5 ♍ 44
- ♆ 23 ♍ 08 ℞
- ⊗ 2 ♎ 03
- 4 ♓ 55 ♃
- 5 ♓ 44
- 28 ♒ 23
- 2 ♒ 4 ☾
- ☊ 13 ♏ 05
- 26 ♏ 05 ♂
- 15 ♐ 29 ♀
- 15 ♑ 4 / 1 ☿ ☉
- 3 ♒ 30
- 16 ♏ 30
- 13 ♐ (IC)
- 7 ♑ 24

                 ☊ The NODES ☋

As stated on page 19, the Nodes are always retrograde,
decreasing at the rate of 3 minutes per day.   Since
Raphael's Ephemeris gives the North Node only, and for
every other day, the South Node will be in the opposite
Sign and they will both be adjusted to the date we are
using, if necessary.   For this chart, the North Node
was given as Scorpio 13:48 on Jan. 21st so that on the
22d (the date we are using) it would be 3 minutes less
or 13:45 as we show it.

FOUNDATION OF THE ASTROLOGICAL CHART

Work for A.M. Chart, E-Long. & N-Lat.

11:10:00 a.m. JST Nov. 11, 1951, 139E45 35N40

```
 11:10:00  am JST Nov. 11th  ....  Japanese Standard Time
+   19:00  Diff. E of 135 E            Tokyo, Japan
 11:29:00  am LMT Nov. 11th
+12:00:00  to previous noon         Nearest Latitude in the
 23:29:00  the Interval             Table of Houses is 36.
     3:54  correction Int.
+15:15:21  Sid. Time, 10th          (10th .. 14:00 Scorp
 38:47:75                           (11th ..  7.7  Sagit
-    1:35  corr EGMT 9:19:00        (12th .. 29.4  Sagit
 38:46:42  more than 24 hrs         ( 1st .. 23:05 Capri
-24:00:00  one sidereal day         ( 2nd ..  4.9  Pisces
 14:46:42  Calculated S. T. .. 36N  ( 3rd .. 14.0  Aries
```

GMT and Constant Log.   Moon
                                     11th   22:57 Aries
   11:29 am LMT Nov 11   10th - 9:56 Aries
 - 9:19 EGMT E-Longit   13:01 = 2657 log.
 - 2:10 a.m. GMT 11th   + 3875 C.L.
   11:60 (subtract)   11th - 5:20 = 6532 log.
    9:50 = 3875 C. Log.   17:37 Aries

```
           (Ascendant 9 23:05    When working the Part of
           (Plus Moon  0 17:37   Fortune, we use the num-
Fortuna   (         = 9 40:42    ber of the preceding Sign
           (Minus Sun 7 17:52    (for Aries, it is 0) for
           ( Gemini (2)22:50     Ascendant, Moon and Sun
                                 The answer takes the num-
                                 ber of the Sign following
```

A. M. Chart, East Longitude & North Latitude   27

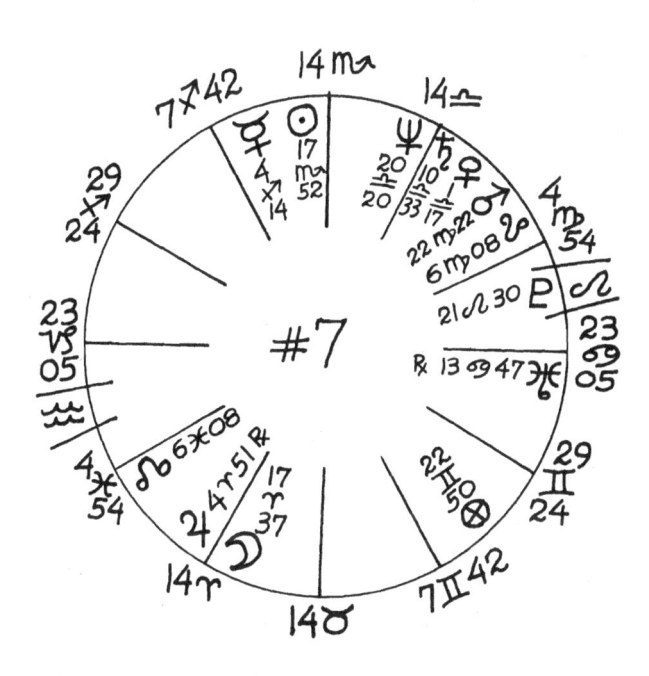

11:10:00 am JST Nov 11 1951   14:46:42 Calc. Sid. Time
 2:10 am GMT 11th = 3875 CL   15:15:21 Sid. Time, 10th

#7

The planet in the Sign

On page 4 herein, refer to the Signs by Quality & Element, etc. Which planets in this chart are in Positive Signs? Which are in Negative Signs? What is meant by these terms? How many planets here are in Fire Signs and how many in Earth? How many are in Air Signs, and how many in Water? What kind of Sign is on the 1st? On page 5, refer to the Planetary Rulership: note that Venus here is in her own Sign. The Sun and Pluto are in "mutual reception" by being in each other's Signs.

FOUNDATION OF THE ASTROLOGICAL CHART

P.M. Chart #8, E-Long. & S-Lat.

7:31 p.m. E. European Time, Feb. 24, 1957, 28E11 25S45

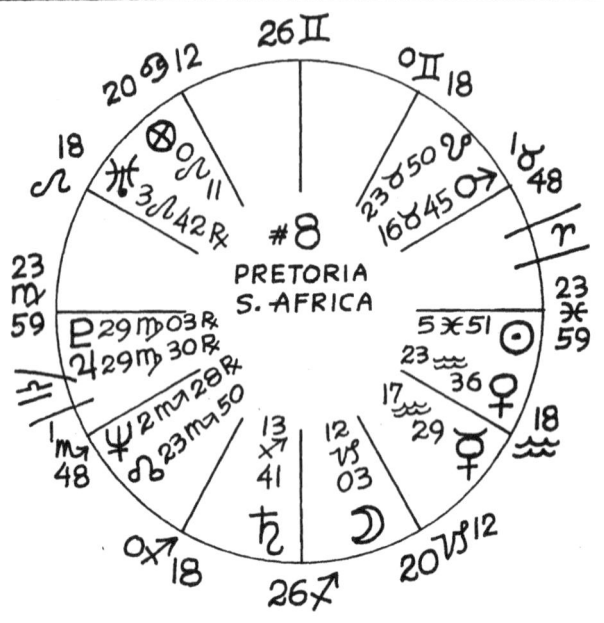

#8 PRETORIA S. AFRICA

```
  7:31:00 pm EET Feb 24th          GMT and Constant Log.
-    7:16  Diff. W of 30 E          7:23:44 pm LMT 24th
  7:23:44 pm LMT-Int 24th         - 1:52:44 EGMT E-Long
     1:13 correction Int.           5:31:00 pm GMT 24th
 22:16:24 Sid. Time, 24th         = .6385 Constant Log.
+12:00:00 for S. Latitude
 41:41:21 Subtract 24 hrs       Moon 25th 21:14 Capricorn
 -24 -0:18 corr EGMT 1:52            24th -9:18 Capricorn
 17:41:03 Calculated S.T.                 11:56 = 3034 log.
 17:42:34 Nearest    (26 S)                   / 6385 C.L.
                                     24th /2:45 = 9419 log.
(Start with the 4th cusp)                12:03 Capricorn
```

A.M. Work, East Longitude & South Latitude 29

(Comparison work for Chart #8, page 28)

00:25:00 a.m. EET Feb. 24, 1957, 28E11, 25S45

00:25:00 am EET Feb 24 1957   22:17:27 Sid. Time, 23rd
10:25 pm GMT 23rd = 3625 CL   22:36:55 Calc. Sid. Time

```
  00:25:00 am EET Feb 24th   ......  Eastern European Time
-  7:16    Diff. W of 30 E           Pretoria, S. Africa
  00:17:44 am LMT Feb 24th
 +12:00:00 preceding noon
  12:17:44 the Interval
      3:02 correction Int.
  22:17:27 Sid. Time, 23rd         (4th .. 7:00  Pisces
 +12:00:00 for S. Latitude         (5th .. 10.2  Aries
  46:36:73 subtract 24 hrs         (6th .. 16.9  Taurus
  -24 -0:18 corr. EGMT 1:52        (7th .. 21:32 Gemini
  22:36:55 Calculated S.T.         (8th .. 15.2  Cancer
  22:34:54 Nearest in Table ... 26S (9th .. 9.3  L e o
```

Using the ADDED LINE

In finding the GMT for EAST Longitude, we subtract the EGMT from the LMT. If the LMT is too small we have to add 12 hours, taking us to the opposite a.m. or p.m. GMT (a p.m. LMT gives an a.m. GMT of the same date, but an a.m. LMT gives a p.m. GMT of the previous date).

GMT and Constant Log.

```
  00:17:44 am LMT 24th
 +12:00:00 to pm, 23rd    the Added Line
  12:17:44 pm LMT 23rd
 - 1:52:44 EGMT E Long.
  10:25:00 pm GMT 23rd = 3625 C. Log.
```

FOUNDATION OF THE ASTROLOGICAL CHART

The LATITUDE of the Planets.

The latitude of the Moon or a planet is its distance north or south of the Sun's path, called the Ecliptic. Since he cannot be north or south of himself, the Sun never has latitude.

Latitude is shown in the ephemeris along with the longitude of the planet (its degree-&-minute in the Sign) and its declination (explained on page 31 herein). It is only a matter of a few minutes for the planets, and can be readily arrived at by mental equation, as we do for the longitude of the slow planets (see page 17).

The Moon's latitude probably never exceeds 5:18, and when the difference is very slight we simply equate it mentally. When the difference is greater, or the latitude is changing in direction, we may wish to calculate it exactly for more precise work, & we then follow the method outlined on page 31 for her declination.

Always set down the GMT-line in detail including the Constant Logarithm. If the latitude is increasing, we work it as we would a direct planet; if decreasing, we work it as we would a retrograde planet. But if it is changing in direction (North on one day & South on the other) we ADD the two places together & change the resulting figure to a log, to which we add the C.L., and then change the resulting log back to time: this is the small motion: if it is smaller than the latitude on the GMT-date we are able to subtract and we do so, marking the answer the same N. or S. direction as the latitude on the GMT-date. If it is larger than the latitude or the GMT-date, subtract that latitude from the small motion instead and mark the answer for the direction opposite the one on the GMT-date, as we did on page 31.

The Moon's DECLINATION

Declination is distance north or south of the Celestial Equator. It may be increasing (LEAVING 0-degrees) decreasing (APPROACHING 0-degrees) or changing in direction (CROSSING 0-degrees). It is NORTH in the first 6 Signs, SOUTH in the last 6. Examine the declination of the Moon in the ephemeris on these points.

ALWAYS set down the GMT-line in detail as given below.

If the Declination is INCREASING on the GMT-date, work it as a DIRECT planet.	9:25 pm GMT Jan 5 (+ 5th) 4063 C.L. Jan 6, 19S15 D " 5,-19:10 0:05 = 2.4594 log + 4063 C.L.
(Pm GMT means plus: Am GMT means minus)	+ 5th, 0:02 = 2.8657 log 19S12 = Decl. Moon

-----

If the Declination is DECREASING on the GMT-date, work it as a RETROGRADE planet.	6:45 pm GMT Dec 8 (+ 8th) 5509 C.L. Dec 9 -15N11 R " 8, 17:22 2:11 = 1.0411 log + 5509 C.L.
(The opposite of what the GMT says to do.)	- 8th, 0:37 = 1.5920 log 16N45 = Decl. Moon

-----

If it is CHANGING on the GMT-date, ADD the places together. SUBTRACT the small motion from the place on the GMT-date: if too great, subtract the PLACE from the MOTION but mark it the OPPOSITE direction.	8:00 am GMT Feb 4 (- 4th) 4771 C.L. Feb 4, 1N06 C " 3, +3S20 4:26 = .7335 log + .4771 C.L. - 4th, 1:29 = 1.2106 log SWITCH -1N06 = GMT place Change 0S23 = Decl. Moon

Correcting the Angles

When we have worked the Calculated Sidereal Time and matched it as nearly as possible in the Table of Houses we are usually near enough to accept the Midheaven and Ascendant as they are. For exactitude, however, it is often desirable to correct these angles and especially when they are just entering or just leaving a Sign.

RULE:

1. Find the Difference between the two Sidereal Times nearest your Calculated Sidereal Time, calling one the GREATER S.T. & the other the LESSER S.T. Reduce this Difference to seconds and mark it "A".

2. Find the Difference between the two Ascendants accompanying these Greater & Lesser S. Times. Reduce this Difference to minutes, & mark it "B/Ascendant". B/Midheaven is always 60 min.

3. Find the Difference between the Lesser S. T. and your Calculated Sidereal Time. Reduce this Difference to seconds and mark it "C".

4. Multiply C by B/Asc & divide by A for D/Asc. Add this D to the Lesser Ascendant. The result is the Corrected Asc/Desc for the chart.

5. Multiply C by B/Midheaven (60') & divide by A for D/MC. Add this D to the Midheaven which accompanied the Lesser S. T. The result is the Corrected MC/IC (4th) for the chart.

On page 33 we give examples in correcting the angles.

Examples 33

Chart #5 page 23, 1:42:53 Calc. S.T., 34 N-Lat

```
Gr ST   1:44:00      Asc  6 Leo 44     M.C.      1:42:53 Calc.
Ls ST   1:40:12       "   5  "  57    (27 Ari)   1:40:12 Ls ST
Diff.    (3)48            0  :  47                (2)41
3' x 60"  180           B/Asc   47                 120
       A  228           B/MC    60              C  161

         161 C
       x  47 B/Asc                     161  C
          1127                       x  60  B/M.C.
           644                    A 228/9660/42' D for MC
     A 228/7567/33' D/Asc

   5 Leo 57 Asc Lesser ST         27 Aries 00 Lesser ST MC
   /    33 D for the Asc          /      42 D for the MC
   6 Leo 30 Corrected ASC         27 Aries 42 Corrected MC
```

Example, page 29, 22:36:55 Calc. S.T., 26 S-Lat

```
Gr ST  22:38:39      Asc 22 Gem 25     M.C.     22:36:55 Calc.
Ls ST  22:34:54       "  21  "  32    (7 Vir)   22:34:54 Ls ST
Diff.    (3)45            0  :  53                (2)01
3' x 60"  180           B/Asc   53                 120
       A  225           B/MC    60              C  121

         121 C
       x  53 B/Asc                     121  C
           363                       x  60  B/M.C.
           605                    A 225/7260/32' D for MC
   \ 225/6413/28'/ D/Asc

  !1 Gem 32 Asc Lesser St          7 Vir 00 Lesser S.T. MC
         29 D for the Asc          /     32 D for the M.C.
  !2 Gem 01 Corrected ASC          7 Vir 32 Corrected M.C.
```

The DECANATES

Each Sign of 30 degrees is divided into 3 decanates, or parts of 10. The 1st Decanate (0 to 10) is always entirely of the nature of the Sign itself, and carries the name of that Sign, as set forth in the Table below.

The 2nd Decanate (10 to 20) colors the nature of the Sign by the sub-influence or vibration of the nature of the next Sign OF THE SAME ELEMENT and is named for it.

The 3rd Decanate (20 to 30) reflects a sub-influence traceable to the nature of the remaining Sign - always of the same element - whose name it bears in addition.

It will be recognized from this diversity that there are 36 decanate-types of individuals, according to the degree of the Sign in which the natal Sun appears.

		0-10	Ari		0-10	Leo		0-10	Sag
FIRE	Aries	10-20	Leo	Leo	10-20	Sag	Sagit	10-20	Ari
		20-30	Sag		20-30	Ari		20-30	Leo
		0-10	Tau		0-10	Vir		0-10	Cap
EARTH	Taurus	10-20	Vir	Vir	10-20	Cap	Capri	10-20	Tau
		20-30	Cap		20-30	Tau		20-30	Vir
		0-10	Gem		0-10	Lib		0-10	Aqu
A I R	Gemini	10-20	Lib	Lib	10-20	Aqu	Aquar	10-20	Gem
		20-30	Aqu		20-30	Gem		20-30	Lib
		0-10	Can		0-10	Sco		0-10	Pi.
WATER	Cancer	10-20	Sco	Sco	10-20	Pi.	Pisces	10-20	Can
		20-30	Pi.		20-30	Can		20-30	Sco

The FACES, Positive & Negative 35

Each 10-degree decanate contains two 5-degree FACES, giving six Faces to each Sign, as listed below. It is easier to remember when we note that the first Face is always Positive in a positive or odd-numbered Sign and always Negative in a negative or even-numbered Sign, & there are always two adjoining Faces that are Positive & two that are Negative. The majority of planets Positive radiate out; Negative, they attract within.

Ari	0-05 P) Ari 5-10 N 10-15 N) Leo 15-20 P 20-25 P) Sag 25-30 N	Leo	0-05 P) Leo 5-10 N 10-15 N) Sag 15-20 P 20-25 P) Ari 25-30 N	Sag	0-05 P) Sag 5-10 N 10-15 N) Ari 15-20 P 20-25 P) Leo 25-30 N
Tau	0-05 N) Tau 5-10 P 10-15 P) Vir 15-20 N 20-25 N) Cap 25-30 P	Vir	0-05 N) Vir 5-10 P 10-15 P) Cap 15-20 N 20-25 N) Tau 25-30 P	Cap	0-05 N) Cap 5-10 P 10-15 P) Tau 15-20 N 20-25 N) Vir 25-30 P
Gem	0-05 P) Gem 5-10 N 10-15 N) Lib 15-20 P 20-25 P) Aqu 25-30 N	Lib	0-05 P) Lib 5-10 N 10-15 N) Aqu 15-20 P 20-25 P) Gem 25-30 N	Aqu	0-05 P) Aqu 5-10 N 10-15 N) Gem 15-20 P 20-25 P) Lib 25-30 N
Can	0-05 N) Can 5-10 P 10-15 P) Sco 15-20 N 20-25 N) Pi. 25-30 P	Sco	0-05 N) Sco 5-10 P 10-15 P) Pi. 15-20 N 20-25 N) Can 25-30 P	Pi.	0-05 N) Pi. 5-10 P 10-15 P) Can 15-20 N 20-25 N) Sco 25-30 P

The ASPECTS

Like any circle, large or small, the Zodiac contains 360 degrees, every one of them in some relationship to the others, and this relationship is mathematical. Our name for it is ASPECT, meaning "to look at each other" and this they can do directly, as in an opposition, or sideways as in a semisextile or sextile, and so forth. The ancients said that the planets "behold" each other when they are in aspect. (It is usually with a smile when the aspect is good - with a frown when it isn't.)

The Opposition ☍

One-half of the circle of 360 degrees measures 180 degrees and these points (for example, the Ascendant and Descendant) are therefore in opposition to each other: 180 degrees apart. It is clear, then, that a planet in any degree of the Zodiac will be in opposition to a planet in the opposite Sign and degree.

On the opposite page, we repeat Chart #4. Note that Saturn in 17:53 Pisces is retrograding to the exact opposition of Neptune in 17:13 Virgo. If the minutes now were exactly the same in both cases as the degrees are this would be a "partile" absolutely-exact opposition. When not partile, an aspect is called "platic."

A certain ORB or leeway on either side of exactitude is permitted, so that a planet may be "applying to" or "separating from" an exact aspect. When one planet is Direct and the other Retrograde, like Neptune & Saturn here, they are in "mutual application" to their aspect. Note that the Moon in 7:37 Pisces is "applying to" the opposition of Neptune in 17:13 Virgo and also "separating from" the opposition of Mars in 1:25 Virgo.

The Aspects, cont'd 37

In determining which planet in an aspect is applying to or separating from another, remember that it is always the faster-moving of the two. WE ALWAYS NAME HIM FIRST. The Moon is the swiftest of all; she moves up to any planet if her degree is going forward to his as Moon-to-Neptune here, & she moves away from any planet if she has left the degree he holds, as Moon-and-Mars.

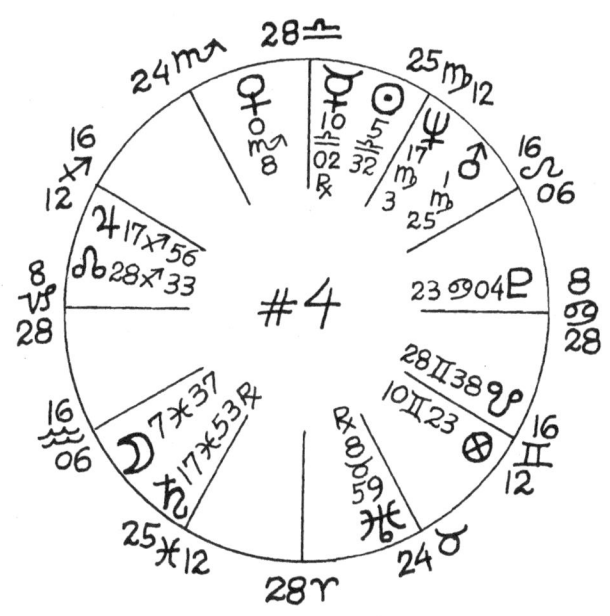

#4

According to their speed of motion, the planets take their places in the following order:

MOON, Mercury, Venus, Sun, Mars,
Jupiter, Saturn, Uranus, Neptune, Pluto.
(See page 5.)

Mercury can apply to or separate from any planet excepting the Moon who is ahead of him in speed. Venus can apply to or separate from any following her, etc.

The Conjunction ☌

Planets are in conjunction when they are within orbs of being in the same degree; usually in the same Sign, but a planet leaving a Sign and one entering the next Sign may be so close to each other by degrees as to be conjunct. (See page 41 for the Table of Orbs.)

Besides being in aspect with each other, planets may also aspect cusps. In Chart #4, note Jupiter conjunct the 12th cusp and Venus conjunct the Midheaven.

The Sextile ⚹

The sextile measures 60 degrees, the distance of two Signs apart like the distance from the 1st cusp to the 3rd. Venus in 0 Scorpio is two Signs away from Mars in 1 Virgo so we say Venus is sextile Mars, naming her first because she is faster than he. The Moon is two Signs away from both Uranus and the Ascendant, and because their degrees are close we say she is sextile to both of them.

The Semisextile ⚺

The semisextile is half a sextile, 30 degrees or the distance from the 1st cusp to the 2nd; one Sign apart. Pluto is semisextile the South Node; the Sun is leaving the semisextile of Mars, and Venus is leaving the semisextile of the Sun.

The Semisquare ∠

The semisquare measures 45 degrees or 15 more than a semisextile; it is the distance of one-and-a-half Signs apart (like the distance from the 1st cusp to the middle of the 2nd House). When Venus reaches 2 Scorpio she will be a Sign and a half from Jupiter and will be exactly semisquare him; as it is, we allow her the orb of 4 degrees and say she is semisquare Jupiter now.

The Square □

The square measures one-fourth of the circle of 360 degrees and is 90 degrees, three Signs apart, the distance from the 1st cusp to the 4th or 10th. Pluto is exactly square the Midheaven, and when Venus was still in Libra she squared Pluto. The Sun is moving forward to square the Ascendant, while Mercury is retrograding back for the same purpose. Note the exact square of Jupiter to both Saturn and Neptune.

The Trine △

The trine measures 120 degrees, four Signs apart, or the distance from the Ascendant to the 5th cusp. It is easiest found when the planets are in the same element as the Moon in 7 Pisces trine Venus in 0 Scorpio (both in Water Signs). Mercury and Fortuna are trine in Air Signs, while Mars and Uranus are trine in Earth Signs.

The Sesquare ⚼

The sesquare measures 135 degrees or 15 more than the trine; it is the distance from the Ascendant to the middle of the 5th House. Venus is sesquare Saturn because he is 17 degrees more than their trine.

The Quincunx ⚻

The quincunx measures 150 degrees, or one whole Sign short of being an opposition. It is the distance from

The Aspects, cont'd

the Ascendant to the 6th House - and also from the 8th House to the Ascendant via the 10th. If Mercury were in Scorpio he would be opposition Uranus but he is one side of an opposition so we say Mercury is quincunx to Uranus. In the same way, the Moon is quincunx the Sun. (The quincunx is sometimes called an "inconjunction".)

The Parallel (of Declination) ‖P

Declination is distance north or south of the Celestial Equator and for the Moon and faster planets it is calculated as given on page 31 herein. Declination is given in the ephemeris along with the longitude and latitude of the planets.

Two planets whose declination is within a degree of being exact are said to be parallel. It is a powerful aspect. When both planets are in North declination or both in South the parallel ranks as a conjunction, but is stronger. When one is North and the other South it is similar to an opposition, but is stronger.

In Chart #4 the Sun in 2S03 and the Moon in 3S41 are in parallel of declination by midnight. Neptune 5N58 and both Saturn & Mercury 6S57 are all three parallel.

Less-commonly-used Aspects

There are five less-commonly-used aspects: the semiquintile, 36 degrees (6 more than the semisextile) and the nonogon, 40 degrees (10 more than the semisextile); the quintile, 72 degrees (12 more than the sextile), the trecile, 108 degrees (18 more than the square) and the biquintile of 144 degrees or 6 less than the quincunx.

The ORB to Allow.

An aspect is exact when both planets involved occupy the identical degree - as in Chart #4 where Jupiter is 17:56 Sagittarius square to Saturn in 17:53 Pisces and also square to Neptune in 17:13 Virgo.

As they approach or leave exactitude the relationship becomes a thing of mathematical measurement and permissible leeway. This leeway on either side of exactitude is called ORB, or the degrees permitted in an aspect that is not exact.

The Sun's orb is 15 degrees; the Moon's, 12; Jupiter & Saturn, 9; Mercury, Venus, Mars, Pluto and Uranus, 7 each, and Neptune, 5.

The Rule is: add the orbs of the two aspecting planets and divide by two, which gives the degrees allowed on either side of the slower planet. However, the following Table is simpler and is altogether acceptable:

Aspect	Planets	Orb
conjunction	together	8
semisextile	30 dg apart	2
semiquintile	36 "	1
nonogon	40 "	1
semisquare	45 "	4
sextile	60 "	8
quintile	72 "	2
square	90 "	8
trecile	108 "	2
trine	120 "	8
sesquare	135 "	4
biquintile	144 "	2
quincunx	150 "	2
opposition	180 "	8

The Syzygies

The syzygy (siz'i-je) refers to the Moon's conjunction to the Sun (New Moon) & her opposition to the Sun (Full Moon) or her conjunction & opposition to a planet. Raphael's Ephemeris lists them on the right-hand pages under the heading "Lunar Aspects".

The Lunation

A lunation is the Moon's conjunction, square or opposition to the Sun (although we usually mean only the New Moon), also the period between one New Moon & the next.

The Eclipse

When the New or Full Moon occurs while her nodes are within 5 degrees of the same Sign and degree, there is a shadow over either the Sun or Moon that eclipses one of them. This is designated on page 29 of Raphael's Ephemeris as ANNULAR (merely a ring on the outer edge) or PARTIAL (incomplete coverage) or TOTAL (entire coverage). The symbol for the conjunction or opposition is blacked out, the meaning of an eclipse. Such a conjunction denotes a SOLAR eclipse (whose effects last 3 years - or as many years as the eclipse lasted hours). The opposition denotes a LUNAR eclipse - whose effects continue for 3 months or as many months as the eclipse lasted hours. In localities where the eclipse is not visible, however, it operates more as a lunation.

The Occultation

When the Moon's conjunction to a planet (not the Sun) eclipses (completely darkens) the planet, it is called an occultation and the conjunction-symbol is blackened.

Finding the Aspects in the Chart 43

Find the aspects here for yourself & check them below.

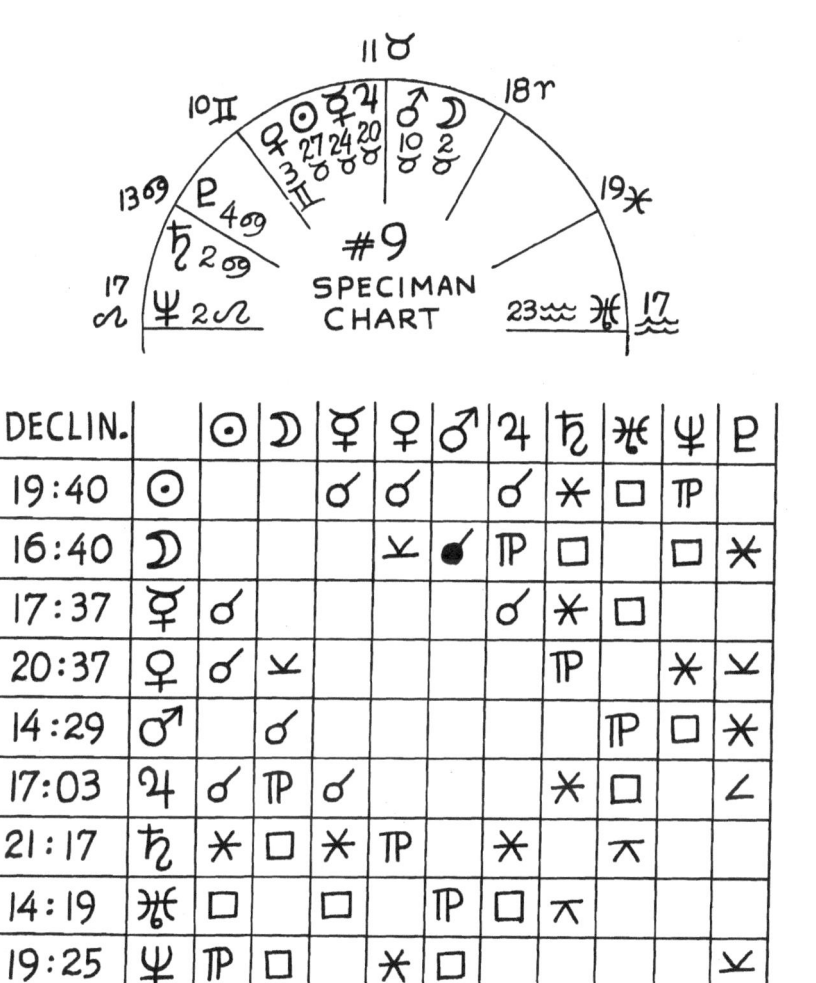

#9 SPECIMAN CHART

Chart positions:
- 11 ♉
- 10 ♊, ☿ 27 ♊, ☉ 24 ♊, ♃ 20 ♊, ♀ 3 ♊
- 18 ♈, ♂ 10 ♉, ☽ 2 ♉
- 13 ♋, ♇ 4 ♋, ♄ 2 ♋
- 19 ♓
- 17 ♌, ♆ 2 ♌
- 23 ♒, ♅ 17 ♒

DECLIN.		☉	☽	☿	♀	♂	♃	♄	♅	♆	♇
19:40	☉			☌	☌	☌	✶	□	℗		
16:40	☽			⊻	●	℗	□		□	✶	
17:37	☿	☌				☌	✶	□			
20:37	♀	☌	⊻				℗		✶	⊻	
14:29	♂	☌		☌				℗	□	✶	
17:03	♃	☌	℗	☌				✶	□		∠
21:17	♄	✶	□	✶	℗		✶		⊼		
14:19	♅	□		□		℗	□	⊼			
19:25	♆	℗	□		✶	□					⊻
23:23	♇		✶		⊻	✶	∠		⊻		

The Midpoints

We find the midpoint between cusps & between angles, between any two planets and between a planet & a cusp. Half the whole distance ∤ the earlier point = midpoint. Remember to allow 12 for the Signs, 30 for the degrees and 60 for the minutes. When subtracting from a lesser Sign add 12; subtract 12 Signs if the answer passes 12. We will use Chart #10, page 45, for the examples below.

Midpoint of 1st House	
S dg mn	
4 12:48	cusp of 2nd House
-3 21:15	cusp of 1st House
0 21:33	whole distance
0 10:46	half the distance
∤3 21:15	cusp of 1st House
4) 2:01	Leo midpoint 1st"

Midpoint of 9th House	
S dg mn	
12 08:00	cusp of the 10th
-11 07:42	cusp of the 9th
1 01:18	whole distance
0 15:39	half the dist.
11 7:42	cusp of the 9th
11)23:21	Pisces mpt of 9th

Midpoint Sun to Moon	
S dg mn	
12 23:13	Moon in Aries
-10 28:59	Sun in Aquarius
1 24:14	the whole dist.
0 27:07	half the dist.
∤10 28:59	Sun's position
11)28:06	Pi mpt Sun/Moon

Midpoint Mercury to 1st	
S dg mn	
15 21:15	Ascendant Cancer
-11 10:51	Mercury in Pisces
4 10:24	the whole dist.
2 5:12	half the dist.
∤11 10:51	Mercury's place
1)16:03	Tau mpt Merc/1st

Midpoint of a Quadrant	
S dg mn	
6 08:00	cusp of 4th House
-3 21:15	cusp of 1st House
2 16:45	whole dist 1st Q.
1 8:22	half 1st Quadrant
∤3 21:15	cusp of 1st House
4)29:37	Leo mpt 1st Quad.

Intercepted Signs
With no intercepted Signs the midpoint of all quadrants have the same degree (the Signs will be square) A quadrant with an intercepted Sign is calculated for itself & its opposite.

The Moon's Aspects in Horary Astrology 45

In Horary Astrology the Moon is the main significator of the activity to take place based on the aspects she APPLIES TO but made only while in the Sign she tenants in the chart. These are to be listed below the wheel.

__Example:__ 2:32:00 p.m. PST Feb. 17, 1953, 118W15 34N

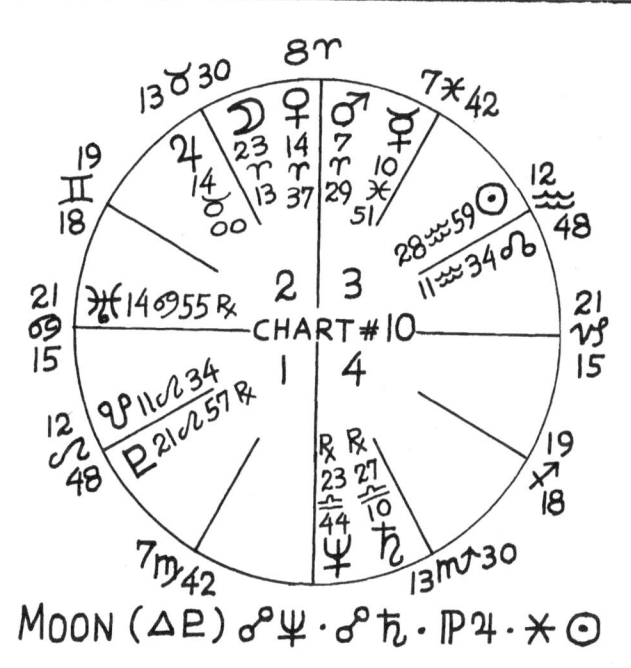

[Chart #10 wheel diagram]

MOON (△♇) ☍♆ · ☍♄ · ▭♃ · ✶☉

(See TABLE for Moon changing Signs, p. 39 Ephemeris.)

The ASPECTARIAN, p. 31 of Raphael's Ephemeris, shows that this Moon 23:13 will be opposition Neptune, 23:44 as her first applying aspect which we list accordingly with those that follow up to 9:51 a.m. Feb. 18th, when she leaves the Sign. Just before her first applying aspect (opposition Neptune) she was trine Pluto, so we put it in parenthesis as separating and in the past.

PROGRESSING the Chart

As time goes on, the original cusps and planets in a chart move through the Signs, thus PROGRESSING to new positions. The original horoscope stamps the fixed promise forever so far as developments in the life are concerned, but everything doesn't happen at once and a developing period is required for the original promise to materialize. Aspects not exact at birth mark an important progressed year when they reach exactitude.

The SECONDARY Method

In the Secondary Method of progression we say that a day of life represents a year of life, as laid down in the Bible. Using the natal ephemeris (and the following one if necessary), the 2nd day of life shows where the planets will be in the 2nd YEAR of life, and so on.

1. The desired year minus the birth year gives the age in DAYS to go forward to find the Progressed Date.
2. For a p.m. birth, take the S.T. for the Prog. Date: for an a.m. birth, take the S.T. for the day before.
3. Find the difference between this new S.T. & the one at birth: mark it Increase, for that many YEARS.
4. To this Increase add the Calc. Sid. Time that gave the original M.C. and mark it Progressed Sid. Time.
5. In the Table of Houses and using the birth Latitude find the Prog. S.T. & the progressed cusps it gives.
6. Progress the planets according to the original GMT line. If p.m., you used the birthdate and the day after: now use the progressed date & the day after. If a.m., you used the birthdate and the day before: now use the progressed date & the day before. Continue to use the original Constant Logarithm.

Progressing Chart #4, page 21, 118W15 34N   47

1:08:00 pm PST Sept 28 1936   12:28:20 Sid. Time, 28th
9:08 pm GMT 28th = .4196 CL   13:44:50 Calc. Sid. Time

Let us progress the chart for age 5 because the Sun's degree-a-year travel will bring him to 10 Libra to the conjunction of Mercury (which he promised originally).

1. 1941 Desired Year
   -1936 Birth Year   The progressed year always
       5 years (DAYS)   begins on the birthday and
   ⧸ 28 Sept (birth)   continues to the next.
      33
   - 30 days in Sept
      3 Oct 1936 = Prog. Date for the planets in 1941

2. 12:48:03 Sid Time Oct 3d   (M.C.   3:00 Scorp.
3. -12:28:20 "   " Sept 28   (11th 28:18 Scorp.
    00:19:43 Increase 5 days   (12th 20:30 Sagit.
4. ⧸13:44:50 Calc. Sid. Time   (ASC: 13:10 Cancer
    14:04:33 Prog. Sid. Time   (2nd   21:48 Aquar.
5. 14:03:08 Nearest in Table - 34N (3rd   00:54 Aries

6. PROGRESSED MOON Sept. 28, 1941 to Sept. 28, 1942

             Oct 4th,   2:03 Gemini (call it 32:03)
             Oct 3rd, -17:19 Taurus
    * Year's Motion   14:44 = 2119 log.
                      ⧸ 4196 C.I.
             Oct 3rd ⧸ 5:36 = 6315 log.
                      23:55 Taurus .... Sept. 1941
                    ⧸ 14:44 Year's Motion
                       8:39 Gemini .... Sept. 1942

* The year's motion 14:44 gives monthly rate of 1:13⧸8

The Moon's Place Month by Month

In Chart #8, p. 49 (repeated from page 28 herein) we look forward to the period when the Moon will conjunct Mars, ruler of the money-2nd in the legacy-8th because her trine to him at birth promised this gain. The natal ephemeris shows that she does this on March 6th, which is 10 days after birth, denoting 10 YEARS after, which points to the period from his birth month February 1967 to February 1968 so we progress the chart accordingly.

The Moon moves from 12:38 Taurus to 24:20 Taurus, at a yearly motion of 12:42 which breaks down to 1:03 ∤ 6 for her monthly motion, as follows:

```
            1 : 03 per month        Add this monthly increase
12 mos/12 : 42 per year             consecutively at the rate
           12                       of 1:03 & 1:04 per month,
         0  36                      alternately (which allows
            6 min. over             for the 6 minutes over).
```

Show the Moon's month-by-month position & her aspects.

```
Moon in Taurus 1967 Feb 12:38 .. trine natal Moon
                    Mch 13:41
                    Apr 14:45 .. sesq Jupiter & Pluto
                    May 15:48
                    Jun 16:52 .. CONJUNCT NATAL MARS
                    Jul 17:55 .. square natal Mercury
                    Aug 18:59
                    Sep 20:02
                    Oct 21:06
                    Nov 22:09           (conj S. Node
                    Dec 23:13 .. CONJUNCT PROG. MARS
               1968 Jan 24:13           (square Venus
                    Feb 25:20           (trine Ascend.
```

PROGRESSED Chart #8 page 28, 28E11 25S45   49

7:31:00 pm EET Feb 24 1957   22:16:24 Sid. Time, 24th
5:31 pm GMT 24th = 6385 CL   17:41:03 Calc. Sid. Time

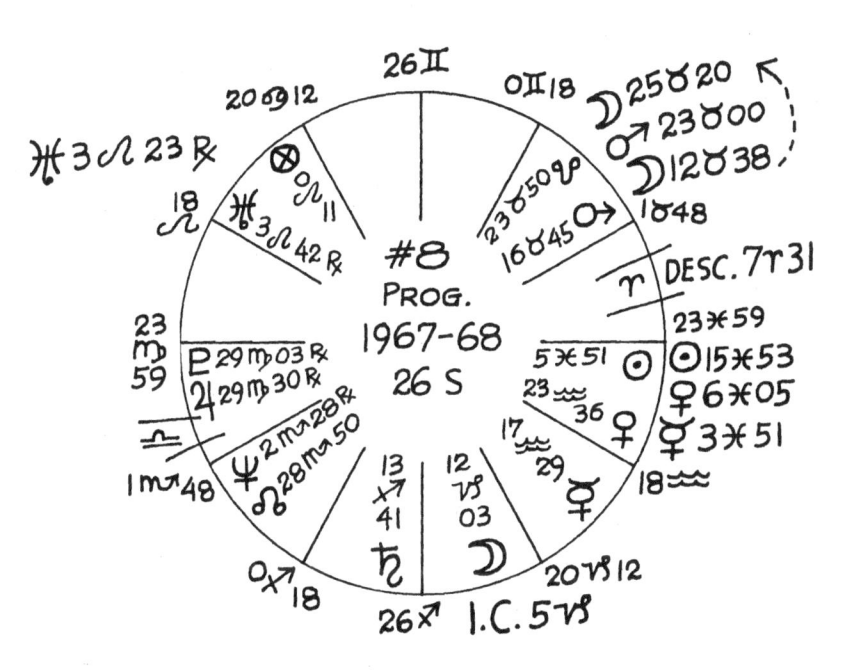

#8 PROG. 1967-68 26 S

22:55:49 Sid Time Mch 6th
22:16:24 " " Feb 24th
00:39:25 Increase 10 days
17:41:03 Calc. Sid. Time
18:20:28 Prog. Sid. Time
18:21:47 Nearest in Table
Lat. 26 S, start with 4th)

ie Moon to conjunct natal
urs June 1967 carries the
rent to Dec. 1967 when she conjuncts progressed Mars.

Moon (1967 to 1968)

7th 22:25 Taurus
6th - 9:43 Taurus
      12:42 = 2764 log.
           / 6385 C.L.
6th / 2:55 = 9149 log.
      12:38 Taur 2/1967
      25:20 Taur 2/1968

Rectifying the Birth Hour

The birth hour is the basis of the Midheaven; if one is not right, the other is not right. If they are correct, the aspects made or received by the Midheaven at the time of an important event will be close to exactitude. But if the progressed M.C. has either passed or not yet reached the degree of the aspect that accounts for the event, we know we have to correct it first and through it reach the correct natal M.C. that will give us the rectified hour of birth. It is very easy to do.

The Midheaven

Note that the Table of Houses gives 360 Midheavens, one for every degree of the Zodiac, each of them being accompanied by its equivalent in Sidereal Time that increases at the rate of 4 minutes for each degree. For every degree the progressed M.C. is off, the natal M.C. is also off, which tells us that the birth hour is off by 4 minutes of time one way or the other. If the M.C. is off by two degrees the birth hour is 8 minutes off. Add or subtract the number of degrees required to bring the progressed M.C. to the exact aspect. This is the correct progressed Midheaven. Add or subtract the same number of degrees to adjust the natal M.C. accordingly.

Find this adjusted natal M.C. in the Table of Houses and take its Sidereal Time as your Calculated Sidereal Time for the chart. The difference between it and the Calculated Sidereal Time you figured originally is the difference to add to or subtract from the original time of birth, thus arriving at the correct time of birth.

Rectifying the Birth Hour, cont'd

Planets in angles will always be aspected by the progressed M.C., which helps to find the correct degrees, as just outlined, when they are being aspected. Among the important events these cover are marriage, divorce or dissolution of partnership, purchase of real estate or a home, deaths in the family, long journeys or voyages, accidents, operations, public recognition, rises in the world, and so on.

The Ascendant

Sometimes it is the Ascendant that is making the aspect without precision and for exactitude should be in an earlier or later degree by progression. In the Table of Houses, and for the latitude of birth, locate the Ascendant as it ought to be for this aspect & note the Midheaven that accompanies it; that is the correct progressed Midheaven.

The difference in degree between the correct M.C. in the Table and your incorrect progressed M.C. tells you how much to add to or subtract from the natal M.C. and then leads you back to the Table of Houses to match it in order to take the Sidereal Time accompanying it for your Calculated Sidereal Time for the chart. The difference between it & your original Calculated Sidereal Time is the difference to add to or subtract from the original time of birth, thus correcting it.

A progressed aspect is more likely to register right on time when it is a conjunction, square or opposition involving planets in angular houses, but less promptly when involving a weak aspect or planets in succeedent houses. The cadent houses allow still more leeway and are more likely to suppress the news until later.

When Planets Change Direction

The year in which a planet changes direction & turns either Direct or Retrograde is usually singled out for importance in the life. Whether in the past or future it is desirable to progress the chart for that year in order to account for what has already happened because of that planet's influence, or to see what is still to take place: either way, it will register very strongly.

Allowing for a lifetime of 90 years we go forward 90 days in the natal ephemeris for the PROGRESSED area, & we also go backward 90 days in the natal ephemeris for the PRE-NATAL area, remembering that in either case we consider the developments to materialize during the 90 years AFTER birth.

The number of days before or after birth showing any planet marked either D or R (Direct or Retrograde.) is taken as the number of years after birth and indicates the native's age thereby, for chart-progression.

Using Chart #8 page 28, we note simply the birthdate Feb. 24, 1957. Going forward 90 days we find no change during February, but Saturn turns R on March 23d which is 27 days after birth or 27 YEARS after, denoting the year 1984 for special significance. Uranus turns D on April 10th, 45 days after birth or age 45. 2002 would therefore be worth progressing. Both Jupiter and Mercury turn D on May 19th at age 84, the year 2041.

Going backward from the birthdate Feb. 24th, we find pre-natal Mercury going D on Jan. 21st, 34 days before birth, pointing to 1991 (34 years AFTER). This is the only pre-natal change. We list the years accordingly as 1984, 1991, 2002 and 2041, for such progression.

Prominent Degrees of the Zodiac

In every branch of astrology (natal, mundane, horary, medical and meteorological) we recognize the importance of certain prominent degrees of the Zodiac that affect for good or ill whatever planet or cusp they conjunct.

The Critical Degrees

The so-called Critical Degrees are derived from the Moon's average daily motion (13:00) through the Signs, starting at 0-Aries and falling out as follows:

0, 13, 26 of Cardinal Signs; 9, 21 Fixed; 4, 17 Common

Natal planets in Critical Degrees (see Jupiter, Saturn & Neptune, Chart #4, p. 37) register more definitely through the whole life. Progressed planets register critically for the year thus marked. The progressed Moon emphasizes the affairs for the month in which she is critical (see October, p. 48) whether or not she is making any direct aspect, herself.

Certain Fixed Stars

The most prominent malefic fixed stars are Antares in 8 Sagittarius, the Ascelli in 6 Leo and the Pleiades in 29 Taurus, which affect the eyesight under certain conditions; Caput Algol in 24 Taurus considered to be the most evil of all fixed stars, & Serpentis in 19 Scorpio marking "the 'curséd degree of the 'curséd Sign". Among the benefic fixed stars, the most prominent are:

```
 7 Gemini - Aldebaron      7 Virgo  - Vindemiatrix
14   "    - Rigel         19   "    - Deneb
19   "    - Bellatrix     14 Capri  - Vega
12 Cancer - Sirius        29   "    - Altair
22 Libra  - Spica          2 Pisces - Fomalhaut
23   "    - Arcturus      22   "    - Markhab
```

The RADIX System

The Sun's motion (or rather, the earth's rate of rotation which gives the impression that the fixed star, the Sun, is moving) is 00:59:08 per day, approximately one degree, which is an arc or part of a circle. This degree-per-day is taken as a degree-per-YEAR, and used in progressing the chart (but say Directing, instead).

This is the Radix System, advanced about forty years ago by Sepharial and later extended by Robson. It has three advantages to recommend it: the slow planets are no longer slow, retrograde planets go forward directly after birth, & no future reference to the ephemeris is required: all because we add the arc to all the cusps, planets & points equally to arrive at their new places. Subtracting the arc results in the CONVERSE position.

The MAJOR Arc

This Solar motion of 00:59 we call the MAJOR Arc, as given for 100 years in the Table on page 55, opposite. To illustrate its use, we will direct from Chart #8 on p. 49 herein for age 10 (Major Arc 9:51) and note what happens to Uranus. (By Secondary Progression he is in Leo 3:23 R, having hardly moved in those ten days.)

Direct		Signs	dg mn	Converse		Signs	dg mn
Uranus	1957	4	3:42	Uranus	1957	4	3:42
Age arc	10 / 0		9:51	Age arc	10 - 0		9:51
Uranus D	1967	(4)	13:33	Uranus C	1967	(3)	23:51
			Leo				Cancer

Directional Uranus at age 10 will be 13:33 Leo trine natal Saturn: Converse Uranus will be 23:51 Cancer aspecting Venus and the Nodes, never achieved otherwise.

The Radix System, cont'd

TABLE of MAJOR ARCS

Age	Arc	Age	Arc	Age	Arc	Age	Arc
1	0:59	26	25:38	51	50:16	76	74:55
2	1:58	27	26:37	52	51:15	77	75:54
3	2:57	28	27:36	53	52:14	78	76:53
4	3:57	29	28:35	54	53:13	79	77:52
5	4:56	30	29:34	55	54:13	80	78:51
6	5:55	31	30:33	56	55:12	81	79:50
7	6:54	32	31:32	57	56:11	82	80:49
8	7:53	33	32:32	58	57:10	83	81:49
9	8:52	34	33:31	59	58:09	84	82:48
10	9:51	35	34:30	60	59:08	85	83:47
11	10:51	36	35:29	61	60:07	86	84:46
12	11:50	37	36:28	62	61:07	87	85:45
13	12:49	38	37:27	63	62:06	88	86:44
14	13:48	39	38:26	64	63:05	89	87:43
15	14:47	40	39:26	65	64:04	90	88:42
16	15:46	41	40:25	66	65:03	91	89:42
17	16:45	42	41:24	67	66:02	92	90:41
18	17:44	43	42:23	68	67:01	93	91:40
19	18:44	44	43:22	69	68:01	94	92:39
20	19:43	45	44:21	70	69:00	95	93:38
21	20:42	46	45:20	71	69:59	96	94:37
22	21:41	47	46:20	72	70:58	97	95:36
23	22:40	48	47:19	73	71:57	98	96:36
24	23:39	49	48:18	74	72:56	99	97:35
25	24:38	50	49:17	75	73:55	100	98:34

Mos--Arc	Mos--Arc	Mos--Arc	Days	Arc
			4 thru 9	1'
1 5'	5 25'	9 44'	10 " 15	2'
2 10'	6 30'	10 49'	16 " 21	3'
3 15'	7 34'	11 54'	22 " 27	4'
4 20'	8 39'	12 59'	28 & over	5'

FOUNDATION OF THE ASTROLOGICAL CHART

The Radix System, cont'd

The MINOR Arc

The Moon's motion of 13-dg 11-mn per day constitutes the MINOR Arc per year, also given for 100 years in the Table on page 57. This arc may be added to the whole chart as we do the Major Arc, but we usually add it to the natal Moon only, resulting in the MINOR Moon.

The MINOR Moon

The MINOR Moon replaces the month-by-month Moon that we use in the Secondary Method (see page 48). The arc of 13:11 is broken down to a monthly increase of 1:06, with 1:05 in the 6th month, as follows:

```
                              Signs   dg mn
Natal Moon, Feb. 1957  ...      9    12:03
∤ Minor Arc, age       9  ...   3    28:35
= MINOR Moon Feb. 1966 ...     (1)   10:38   Taurus  Feb. 1966
                              ∤ 1:06
                                11:44    "    Mar.    "
                              ∤ 1:06
                                12:50    "    Apr.    "
                              ∤ 1:06
                                13:56    "    May     "
                              ∤ 1:06
                                15:02    "    June    "
                              ∤ 1:06
                                16:08    "    July    "
                              ∤ 1:05
                                17:13    "    Aug.    "
Minor Moon Taurus 10:38       ∤ 1:06
∤ 1 year's motion 13:11         18:19    "    Sep.    "
= Feb 1967 Taurus 23:49 .......  23:49   "    Feb. 1967
```

The Radix System, cont'd

TABLE of MINOR ARCS

Yr	S dg mn	Yr	S dg mn	Yr	S dg mn	Yr	S dg mn
1	0 13:11	26	11 12:35	51	10 12:00	76	9 11:24
2	0 26:21	27	11 25:46	52	10 25:10	77	9 24:35
3	1 09:32	28	0 08:56	53	11 08:21	78	10 07:46
4	1 22:42	29	0 22:07	54	11 21:32	79	10 20:56
5	2 05:53	30	1 05:18	55	0 04:42	80	11 04:07
6	2 19:03	31	1 18:28	56	0 17:53	81	11 17:17
7	3 02:14	32	2 01:39	57	1 01:03	82	0 00:28
8	3 15:25	33	2 14:49	58	1 14:14	83	0 13:38
9	3 28:35	34	2 28:00	59	1 27:24	84	0 26:49
10	4 11:46	35	3 11:10	60	2 10:35	85	1 10:00
11	4 24:56	36	3 24:21	61	2 23:46	86	1 23:10
12	5 08:07	37	4 07:32	62	3 06:56	87	2 06:21
13	5 21:18	38	4 20:42	63	3 20:07	88	2 19:31
14	6 04:28	39	5 03:53	64	4 03:17	89	3 02:42
15	6 17:39	40	5 17:03	65	4 16:28	90	3 15:53
16	7 00:49	41	6 00:14	66	4 29:39	91	3 29:03
17	7 14:00	42	6 13:25	67	5 12:49	92	4 12:14
18	7 27:10	43	6 26:35	68	5 26:00	93	4 25:24
19	8 10:21	44	7 09:46	69	6 09:10	94	5 08:35
20	8 23:32	45	7 22:56	70	6 22:31	95	5 21:45
21	9 06:42	46	8 06:07	71	7 05:31	96	6 04:56
22	9 19:53	47	8 19:17	72	7 18:42	97	6 18:07
23	10 03:03	48	9 02:28	73	8 01:53	98	7 01:17
24	10 16:14	49	9 15:39	74	8 15:03	99	7 14:28
25	10 29:25	50	9 28:49	75	8 28:14	100	7 27:38

Mo	dg mn	Mo	dg mn	Da	mn	Da	mn	Da	mn	Da	mn
1	1:06	7	7:41	1	02	7	15	13	28	19	40	25	53
2	2:12	8	8:47	2	04	8	17	14	30	20	42	26	55
3	3:18	9	9:53	3	06	9	19	15	32	21	45	27	57
4	4:24	10	10:59	4	08	10	21	16	34	22	47	28	59
5	5:29	11	12:05	5	11	11	23	17	36	23	49	29	62
6	6:36	12	13:11	6	13	12	25	18	38	24	51	30	64

Directing the Radix Chart

Rate of Progression & ORB

The cusps & planets move forward at the rate of 1 degree per year (60 minutes) or 5 minutes per month. The major directions are operative over a two-year period, because we allow an orb of 1 degree before culmination and 1 degree after.

The Oblique Ascendant

Adding the Major Arc to the Natal Midheaven & Ascendant gives the Directional Midheaven & Ascendant, which may be shown outside the wheel as usual. In the Table of Houses find the M. C. nearest the Directional M. C. and take the Ascendant accompanying it (under the original latitude); this is called the Oblique Ascendant & it is also shown outside the wheel.

```
                                       S   dg mn
Chart   Natal M. C. Feb. 1957 ..  2   26:00
 #8    ≠ Major Arc age    12   ..  0   11:50
        Directional M.C. 1969  ..  3)  7:50  Cancer DIR/MC

Table of Houses MC 8 Cancer (26 S)    7:50  Libra OBL/ASC
```

The Oblique Fortuna

The Oblique Ascendant plus the Directional Moon, then minus the Directional Sun gives the Oblique Fortuna.

```
   The Oblique Ascendant    6    7:50
 ≠ Directional Moon         9   23:50
                           15   30:100
 - Directional Sun         11   17: 41
 = The Oblique Fortuna     4) 13:59  Leo OBL/Fortuna
```

Directing the Chart, cont'd

CONVERSE Directing

As demonstrated on page 54 for Uranus, we add the arc to find the DIRECT Direction but we subtract the arc to find the Converse Direction. We do this for any cusp, planet or point, and we also find the Converse Oblique Ascendant (after finding the Converse Midheaven).

Converse M.C. & Oblique Ascendant

```
Chart   Natal M.C. Feb. 1957 ..  2  26:00
 #8     - Major Arc age   14  ..  0  13:48
        = Converse M.C.  1971 ..  2) 12:12 Gemini CON/MC
                                  12:30 Virgo C/O/ASC
```

M.C. 12 Gemini in Table of Houses (26S) is accompanied by 12:30 Virgo for the **Converse Oblique Ascendant**, and this is trine Natal Moon in the 4th, denoting an unexpected but beneficial development in the home circle.

The Converse MINOR Moon

```
Natal Moon Feb. 1957 ...  9  12:03
- Minor Arc age   12  ...  5  08:07
Conv Minor Moon 1969 ...  4)  3:56 Leo C/M/Moon
```

This Conv/Minor Moon in Feb. 1969 (age 12) passes over Natal Uranus square Neptune, a disruptive influence in the 11th (circumstances out of his control) and in the 2nd (possessions, holdings, finances, etc.).

Find the month-by-month position of the Converse Minor Moon by subtracting 1:06, the monthly **decrease**. She conjuncts Uranus in Feb. 1969, squares Neptune in March and conjuncts Fortuna in May, then leaves the Sign and in 29 Cancer in June 1969 sextiles Jupiter and Pluto.

FOUNDATION OF THE ASTROLOGICAL CHART

Directing the Chart, cont'd

Mundane Parallels

By MUNDANE we refer to the houses of the chart. For parallels we particularly use the cusps of the angular houses, the M.C. and I.C. (4th) and the ASC. and DESC.

Picture the design of a parallel as formed by a line (either the meridian or horizon) with a planet on each side, each the same distance from the line. One planet may be there at birth and the other move up by progression to arrive at that point the same distance from the line ON THE OTHER SIDE to form the parallel.

MP ... When two planets are the same distance from the MC or IC on opposite sides they are in Meridian Parallel (MP). In Chart #8, Saturn is 12-dg from the I.C.; this added to the I.C. marks his parallel point Capricorn 8:19, a distance of 3:44 from the Moon. Roughly, 3:44 is the equivalent of 4 years (see Table, page 55) to be reached by the Converse Moon in 1961 forming her Meridian Parallel to Saturn.

HP ... When two planets are the same distance from the ASC or DESC on opposite sides they form the Horizontal Parallel (HP). In Chart #8, the Sun is 18:08 from the DESC; this added to the DESC takes him to 12:07 Aries, his parallel point. Directional Venus will reach this point in a distance of 48-dg 31-min to form the Horizontal Parallel to the Sun around age 49 (Table p. 55).

RP ... When either the Meridian or Horizon reaches the midpoint between two planets, we again have our design of a line with a planet on either side. This is called a Rapt Parallel (RP). In Chart #8 the midpoint between

Directing the Chart, cont'd

Saturn and Venus falls in 18:38 Capricorn - a distance of 22-dg 38-min from the I.C. and equivalent to age 23 for the Directed I.C. to form the Rapt Parallel between Saturn and Venus in the year 1980, as follows:

Midpoint Saturn to Venus		
10 23:36	Venus in Aquarius	
-8 13:41	Saturn in Sagit.	
2 09:55	whole distance	
1 04:57	half the distance	
/8 13:41	Saturn's position	
9)18:38	Capri mpt Sat/Ven	

Midpoint ..	9 18:38	
- the IC ..	8 26:00	
Distance ..	0 22:38	
22:38 = age		23
/ birth year		1957
IC RP Sat/Ven		1980

QP ... When a planet reaches the same distance from the Meridian that another already is from the Horizon - or vice versa - they form a square design called the Quadrate Parallel. In Chart #8 the Sun is 18:08 from the Horizon: the I.C. (Meridian) in 26:00 Sagittarius minus 18:08 gives the quadrate point 3:52 Sagittarius. For Saturn to back up from 13:41 Sagittarius to 3:52 Sagittarius by Converse motion gives a difference of 9:49 & points to age 10 (Table, p. 55) or 1967, when Converse Saturn will be in Quadrate Parallel with the Sun.

DP ... This is the Directional Parallel, formed by the MINOR Moon. Note the distance from a Directional angle to a natal planet & subtract that distance from the Directional angle, which gives the place of the parallel point on the other side (for the Minor Moon to reach):

Natal M.C. 1957 .. 2 26:00
/ Arc age   8 .. 0 7:53
Dir/M. C. 1965 .. 3) 3:53 Cancer (semisextile Uranus)

3 03:53 Dir/M.C.
- 30:00 to Uran.
3) 3:53 Gemini, Par/Pt

When the Minor Moon reaches the parallel point 3:53 Gem she will be in DP with Uran.

FOUNDATION OF THE ASTROLOGICAL CHART

The Nodal Points

The nodal points of the planets are nearly constant, moving not more than 1½ degrees in a hundred years, so that their positions in 1932 are still operative. The S. Nodes are directly opposite the N. Nodes given here.

Planet	N. Node	Tendency	Vibration
Mercury	17 Taurus	Literary	Mental
Venus	14 Gemini	Artistic	Social
Mars	12 Taurus	Mechanical	Physical
Jupiter	9 Cancer	Academic	Educational
Saturn	27 Cancer	Vocational	Ambitious
Uranus	12 Gemini	Inventive	Scientific
Neptune	12 Leo	Idealistic	Spiritual
Pluto	20 Cancer	Isolating	Separative
Moon	Ephemeris	Instinctual	Functional

Natal planets on these nodes respond through life to their innate tendencies & vibrational self-expression.

Progressed Sun & ruler Ascendant on these nodes will reflect such tendencies and vibrational expression for the time being. Allow one degree orb before & after.

SOLAR HOUSES and TRANSITS

The Solar Chart is one in which the rising Sign must always be the native's Sun Sign. The remaining Signs follow around in their natural order, designating what we call Solar Houses. That is, the Sign following the Sun Sign designates the Solar 2nd House; the next Sign marks the Solar 3rd House, and so on around the wheel. No degrees or natal planets are used, nor do we do any calculating of any kind. It is simply a SIGN Chart.

The purpose of the Solar Chart is to know which mundane (House) affairs are being activated by transiting planets going through these houses. We keep the chart as a framework for current transits, so to speak - but we make it personal by turning a natural transit-wheel (with Aries rising) so that our personal Sun Sign will fall on the Ascendant, if we are not born under Aries.

Transits come from the current ephemeris and are outsiders, not related to us like our natal and progressed planets. They bring OUTSIDERS into our circle and affect us through their affairs more than our own. They are the people who knock at our door asking directions or delivering packages, requesting contributions, favors or assistance, and so on.

On the surface this may seem unimportant and lacking in lasting impact, but to the serious astrologer these transits account for day-to-day developments that must be recognized simply because they take place. We are in touch with the outside world and outsiders; this is a simple way to evaluate such contacts.

The student should know which houses rule which matters, therefore, and expect those matters to be activated by transits; for long periods, under slow planets.

FOUNDATION OF THE ASTROLOGICAL CHART

Your PRESENT-AGE Natal Planet

The natal planet representing your age for any given year-between-birthdays influences by its nature whatever progressions are in force at the time, whether or not the age-planet itself is included in them. In this connection, each planet has its number, as in Table I:

TABLE I ..
1 - Sun	4 - Saturn	7 - Mercury
2 - Moon	5 - Mars	8 - Uranus
3 - Venus	6 - Jupiter	9 - Neptune

Your last birthday plus your next, then reduced to a single digit, gives one of the numbers in Table I, and thus tells you which planet in your natal chart is the influencing one during the period between those birthdays. For example, age 21 plus 22 gives 43, which reduces to 7 (4 ∤ 3) and points to Mercury in your chart. Developments in your life during his periods will bear his stamp, involving much coming-&-going, conversation or writing, some documents or tickets, and so on. See the text for Vice-President Nixon's chart, page 65. If the planet rules or is in an angle it is personal.

TABLE II (Ages)

1 Sun	0/1	9/10	18/19	27/28	36/37	45/46	54/55	63/64
3 Ven	1/2	10/11	19/20	28/29	37/38	46/47	55/56	64/65
5 Mars	2/3	11/12	20/21	29/30	38/39	47/48	56/57	65/66
7 Merc	3/4	12/13	21/22	30/31	39/40	48/49	57/58	66/67
9 Nept	4/5	13/14	22/23	31/32	40/41	49/50	58/59	67/68
2 Moon	5/6	14/15	23/24	32/33	41/42	50/51	59/60	68/69
4 Sat	6/7	15/16	24/25	33/34	42/43	51/52	60/61	69/70
6 Jup	7/8	16/17	25/26	34/35	43/44	52/53	61/62	70/71
8 Uran	8/9	17/18	26/27	35/36	44/45	53/54	62/63	71/72

Your Present-Age Planet, cont'd   65

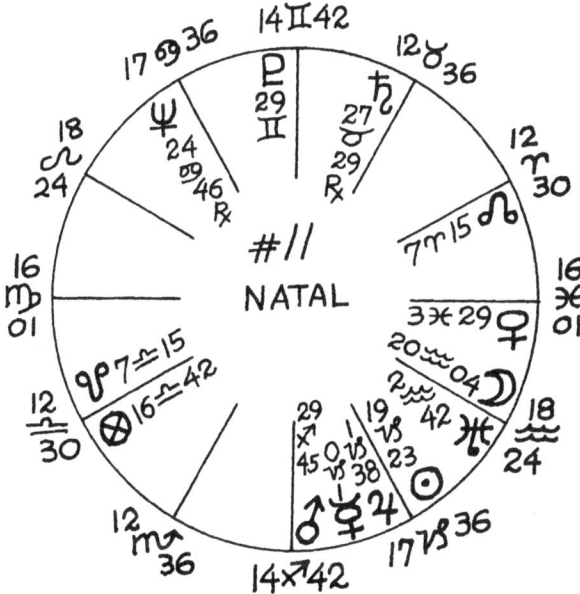

Richard Nixon   9:30 p.m. PST
118W15 & 34N   Jan. 9, 1913

Mr. Nixon was elected Vice-President of the U. S. A.
on Nov. 4, 1952, his age between 39 and 40, which adds
up to 79 & reduces to 16 then to 7, indicating Mercury
as present-age planet between those birthdays. Mercury
will always be significant for Mr. Nixon because it is
ruler of the man himself (Ascendant) & his career (Midheaven) conjunct Jupiter-of-Titles in an angular house
which is a PROMISE at birth, sure of fulfillment.

In 1952 Mercury moved to 1:57 Pisces sextile Jupiter
bringing that fulfillment to his own present-age-year.
The other progressions in 1952 accounting for developments in his career were Venus 14:52 Aries sextile the
Midheaven, the Sun 28 Aquarius trine Pluto in the Midheaven, & Moon 16 Cancer in the 10th sextile the Asc.

FOUNDATION OF THE ASTROLOGICAL CHART

The Solar Return

On or about your birthday each year, the Sun in the CURRENT ephemeris comes back to his place in your natal chart accompanied by the transits that day, thus forming the Solar Return Chart to last for the year ahead. Always set down the birth data as at the top of page 67.

1. Using the Table on p. 68, add the age-equivalent to your Natal Calculated Sidereal Time to arrive at the Sidereal Time for your Solar Return Chart. The S. T. nearest to this in the Table of Houses under the latitude of the locality you are in ON YOUR BIRTHDAY gives the Solar Return cusps.

2. This Solar Return Sidereal Time minus your natal LMT gives the Solar LMT: if the Sun Sign is in an a.m. house in the Solar wheel, the Solar LMT will be a.m.: otherwise, it is p.m. Mark it and date it. The Sun nearest to your natal Sun will be between two noons in the current ephemeris — the earlier date goes on a p.m. LMT, while the later date goes on an a.m. LMT. See Step 2, page 67.

3. Add the EGMT for the locality you are in on your birthday if in West Longitude: if East, subtract. This gives the GMT: mark it a.m. or p.m. and date it: take its Constant Log. as usual. Calculate the Sun, Moon & any fast planet changing Signs.

Read the Solar chart to the natal chart as on page 69, to ascertain the developments to expect during the year. We use only applying aspects, allowing a 5-degree orb. Any planets angular in the Solar Chart bring the matters they rule in the natal chart right out into the open.

Solar Return 1952 for Chart #11, p. 65   67

9:37 pm LMT Jan 9 1913 118W15 34N (4:53:34 Calc. S.T.)

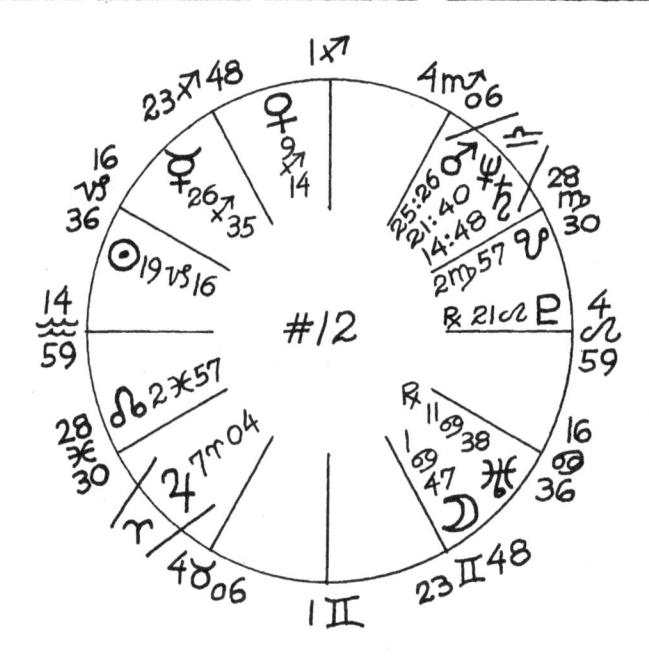

[Chart #12 with the following placements:]
- 1 ♐ (MC)
- 23 ♐ 48
- 16 ♑ 36
- ☿ 26 ♐ 35
- ♀ 9 ♐ 14
- ☉ 19 ♑ 16
- 14 ♒ 59
- 28 ♓ 30
- ♄ 2 ♓ 57 (and ♆ nearby)
- ♃ 27 ♈ 04 ♂ 2 ♈ 57
- 4 ♉ 06
- 1 ♊ (IC)
- 23 ♊ 48
- ☽ 1 ♋ 47, ♅ 11 ♋ 38 ℞
- 16 ♋ 36
- 4 ♌ 59, ♇ 21 ♌ ℞
- 28 ♍ 30
- ♂ 0 ♎, ♆ 21:40, ♄ 14:48 (25:26 group)
- 4 ♏ 06

Sun between Jan 10 & 11   (M.C. .. 1:00 Sagit
(Natal Sun 19:23 Capri)   (11th .. 23.8 Sagit
                               (12th .. 16.6 Capri
.. 11:02:00 equiv. age 39   (ASC: .. 14:59 Aquar
 ∤ 4:53:34 Natal Calc ST   (2nd .. 28.5 Pisces
   15:55:34 Solar Calc ST 34 N (3rd .. 4.1 Taurus

!. - 9:37:00 natal LMT   SUN
     6:18:34 Sol-LMT am 11th..11th 20:12 Capricorn
 '.∤ 7:53:00 EGMT W-Longit   10th 19:11 Capricorn
    14:11:00 past midnight   1:01 = 13730 log.
   -12:00:00 midnight BACK   ∤ 10411 C.L.
     2:11:00 pm GMT Jan 10th..10th ∤0:05 = 24141 log.
           = 1.0411 C. Log   19:16 Capricorn

SOLAR RETURN TABLE
For Age-Equivalent in Time

(Yearly rate 5-hrs 49-min)

Age	Hr Mn	Age	Hr Mn	Age	Hr Mn
1 =	5:49	31 =	12:28	61 =	19:05
2	11:38	32	18:17	62	0:54
3	17:28	33	0:06	63	6:44
4	23:17	34	5:55	64	12:33
5	5:06	35	11:45	65	18:22
6	10:55	36	17:34	66	0:11
7	16:45	37	23:23	67	6:01
8	22:34	38	5:12	68	11:50
9	4:23	39	11:02	69	17:39
10	10:12	40	16:51	70	23:28
11	16:02	41	22:40	71	5:18
12	21:51	42	4:29	72	11:07
13	3:40	43	10:19	73	16:56
14	9:29	44	16:08	74	22:45
15 =	15:19	45 =	21:57	75 =	4:35
16	21:08	46	3:46	76	10:24
17	2:57	47	9:36	77	16:13
18	8:46	48	15:25	78	22:02
19	14:36	49	21:14	79	3:52
20	20:35	50	3:03	80	9:41
21	2:14	51	8:53	81	15:30
22	8:03	52	14:42	82	21:19
23	13:53	53	20:31	83	3:09
24	19:43	54	2:20	84	8:59
25	1:32	55	8:10	85	14:48
26	7:21	56	13:59	86	20:57
27	13:11	57	19:48	87	2:27
28	19:00	58	1:37	88	8:16
29	0:49	59	7:27	89	14:05
30 =	6:38	60 =	13:16	90 =	19:54

Reading Solar Chart #12 to Natal Chart #11

In 1952, Mr. Nixon was elected Vice-President of the United States, a signal honor seen by the Solar Ascendant trine the natal Midheaven while the natal Ascendant appears in the Solar 7th (publicity) which shows where the personal affairs will function for the period. To further emphasize career matters, the progressed ruler of the natal 10th, Mercury in 1:57 Pisces, received the exact trine of the functioning Solar Moon 1:47 Cancer.

His personal income tax matters came to unfavorable, politically-inspired public criticism, as shown by the Solar Venus, ruler of the natal financial-2nd House, in an angle (public attention) in opposition to the natal Midheaven (reputation). However, interceptions in the Solar 2nd (what you own) and Solar 8th (what you owe) show such matters suppressed to his advantage (Jupiter rising protects the person). Also, the ruler of the natal 12th now in the Solar 12th succeeds in suppressing private affairs by keeping them there.

The ruler of his natal 4th (real estate) in the ownership-2nd but intercepted indicates by trine to Venus who rules his natal 2nd that he will buy a home during the year, perhaps a little later. The Solar Moon is interested in a home when in Cancer but her opposition to Jupiter in the natal home-4th separates her from an existing home-address for the time she has to wait for her trine to natal Venus to materialize new ownership.

Solar Mars in this 8th brings the ruler of the natal 8th into the department of death; square natal Neptune in the 11th (the death-8th from the family-4th) denotes the passing of a member of the family, but deferred to a later year because of the interception - which holds developments in abeyance. (His father died in 1956.)

The Lunar Return

Unlike the work on the Solar Return, where we wait a year for the Sun to come back to his natal position and then use the current ephemeris each time, the Moon comes back to her natal position each month after birth & we use the natal ephemeris & those immediately following. The 2nd month represents her return the 2nd year, etc.

The natal Moon's Sign, degree, month & its date, are the basis for the Lunar Return Table, as shown for the first entry below which happens to begin with January. The age in years added to the birth year gives the progressed year, but taken as MONTHS & added to the birth year it tells which EPHEMERIS to use (see p. 71). In that ephemeris, take the month on line with the age in the Table, find the date when the Moon matches the natal Moon, take her accompanying planets unworked, and read them to the natal chart to see what is ahead that year.

(For Chart #13, p. 71)
PERMANENT TABLE FOR THE LUNAR RETURN

Moons					Return
25 Scorp.	on Jan 15	age	1, 13, 25, 37, 49, 61, 73, 85
25 Sagit.	" Feb 15	"	2, 14, 26, 38, 50, 62, 74, 86
25 Capri.	" Mar 15	"	3, 15, 27, 39, 51, 63, 75, 87
25 Aquar.	" Apr 15	"	4, 16, 28, 40, 52, 64, 76, 88
25 Pisces	" May 15	"	5, 17, 29, 41, 53, 65, 77, 89
25 Aries	" Jun 15	"	6, 18, 30, 42, 54, 66, 78, 90
25 Taurus	" Jul 15	"	7, 19, 31, 43, 55, 67, 79, 91
25 Gemini	" Aug 15	"	8, 20, 32, 44, 56, 68, 80, 92
25 Cancer	" Sep 15	"	9, 21, 33, 45, 57, 69, 81, 93
25 Leo	" Oct 15	"	10, 22, 34, 46, 58, 70, 82, 94
25 Virgo	" Nov 15	"	11, 23, 35, 47, 59, 71, 83, 95
25 Libra	" Dec 15	"	12, 24, 36, 48, 60, 72, 84, 96

Man's Natal Chart and 1942 Lunar Return   71

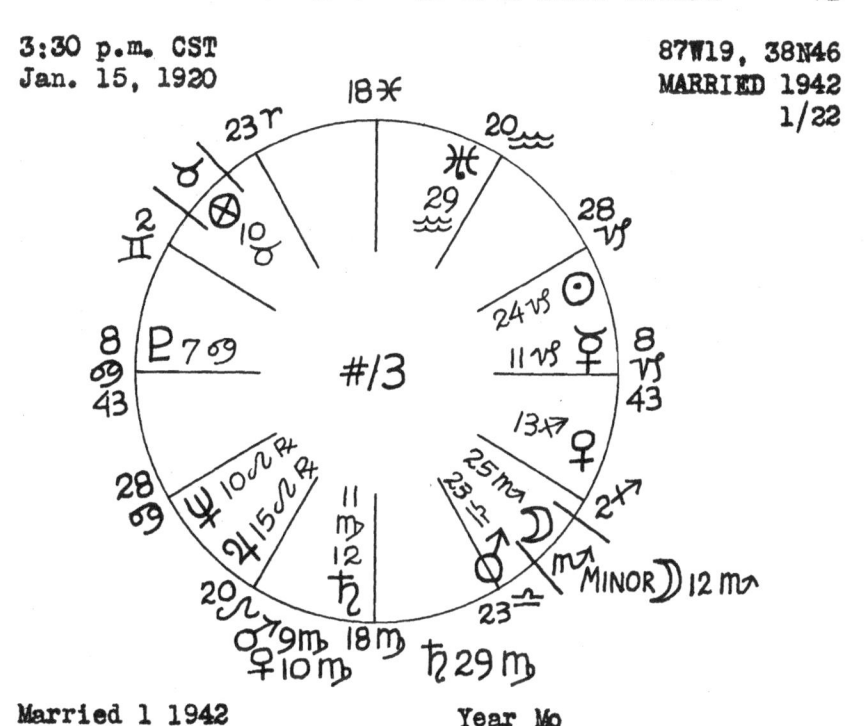

3:30 p.m. CST   87W19, 38N46
Jan. 15, 1920   MARRIED 1942
                                                    1/22

Married 1 1942   Year Mo
Born   1 1920   1920
Age ... 0 22 = 22 months = 1 10
              Ephemeris = 1921 10 = Return Oct. 4th

LUNAR CONSTANT
This is the difference between the natal Moon's degree
and date: here, it is forever 10 (25-15). It is used
to find the MINOR Moon (headed "Moons" in the Table) on
the date of the MONTH of an event. Married in January,
his Minor Moon will be in Scorpio: the date 22d, minus
his Lunar Constant 10 gives his Minor Moon 12 Scorpio,
sextile Saturn ruler marriage-7th, and sextile Mercury
in the 7th. Note Saturn quincunx Uranus in the ritual-
9th. Venus & Mars co-rulers of the love-5th, conjunct
Saturn & trine Fortuna & the 7th House & Mercury there.

The Johndro Locality Charts

A locality chart is one set for only a place & date, without reference to clock time. When set for a place of birth in particular it is a BIRTH Locality Chart & of great importance to its owner - even though he also possesses a regular natal chart.

The outstanding exponent and developer of this method was L. Edward Johndro whose book "Earth in the Heavens" is highly recommended to the serious student of astrology. There he will find the delineation, etc., we are not including in this textbook, since we are confining ourselves mainly to the mathematics of the science.

Since clock time is not employed, the usual Sidereal Time is not used. Instead, the figuring is done easily with Right Ascension. The great circle of 360 degrees (ecliptic) that the Sun traverses begins at 0 Aries 0, and Right Ascension is simply distance from 0 Aries 0, measured along the Celestial Equator as we show here:

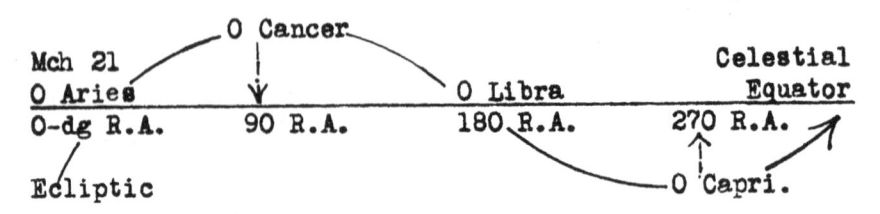

```
                    0 Cancer
Mch 21                                          Celestial
0 Aries             ↓           0 Libra          Equator
0-dg R.A.          90 R.A.     180 R.A.         270 R.A.
                                                    ↑
Ecliptic                                        0 Capri.
```

In Dalton's Table of Houses note that each degree of the Zodiac given for the M.C. in Sidereal Time is also given in Right Ascension called Arc (part of a circle) and it is this Arc that we use in this work. Our only figuring is in finding the Midheaven. The planets are taken as at noon on the birth date and set in the BIRTH Locality & other Locality Charts without calculation.

Johndro Locality Charts, cont'd

Right Ascension advances the M.C. at the rate of 46.10 seconds per year. As an example, correct a difference of 22 years by multiplying by 46.10" & dividing by 60" to get the difference in minutes. Compare with Table.

```
           46.10"
         x   22  years
           99.20
          922.0
    60"/1014.20/16/ or 17'
         60
        414.
        360
         54.20 more than half
```

46.10" CORRECTION TABLE

Yrs	Dif	Yrs	Dif	Yrs	Dif	Yrs	Dif	Yrs	Dif
1	00'	19	15'	37	28'	55	42'	73	56'
2	02'	20	15'	38	29'	56	43'	74	57'
3	02'	21	16'	39	30'	57	44'	75	58'
4	03'	22	17'	40	31'	58	45'	76	58'
5	04'	23	18'	41	32'	59	45'	77	59'
6	05'	24	18'	42	32'	60	46'	78	60'
7	05'	25	19'	43	33'	61	47'	79	61'
8	06'	26	20'	44	34'	62	48'	80	62'
9	07'	27	21'	45	35'	63	48'	81	62'
10	08'	28	22'	46	35'	64	49'	82	63'
11	08'	29	22'	47	36'	65	50'	83	64'
12	09'	30	23'	48	37'	66	51'	84	65'
13	10'	31	24'	49	38'	67	52'	85	65'
14	11'	32	25'	50	38'	68	52'	86	66'
15	12'	33	25'	51	39'	69	53'	87	67'
16	12'	34	26'	52	40'	70	54'	88	68'
17	13'	35	27'	53	41'	71	55'	89	68'
18	14'	36	28'	54	42'	72	55'	90	69'

FOUNDATION OF THE ASTROLOGICAL CHART

Johndro completed his work in 1930 and used that year as the Base Year; the date March 21st for the beginning of the astrological year; the place Greenwich, England for the beginning of Longitude; and 29:10 R.A. for the Midheaven there, as it was at that time. Always set this data down complete as in Line 1, page 75. Only 3 steps are required: to change the year, date and place to suit the person whose chart it is.

The Right Ascension of the Sun

In the Table of Houses, find a Midheaven in the same Sign and degree as the Sun; the Arc accompanying it is the R.A. of the Sun; and if he has minutes, add them.

The 3-step method to follow.

1. Find Difference between Base Year and Birth Year: Multiply that difference by 46.10" & div. by 60": If before 1930, subtract it from 29:10, otherwise add it to 29:10.   NOW YOU HAVE CHANGED THE YEAR.
2. Always add the Ra/Sun's place on the desired day.
   NOW YOU HAVE CHANGED THE DATE.
3. Subtract birthplace Longitude if WEST (add 360:00 if necessary in order to do it); add Longitude if EAST. For S. Latitude, add 180:00. If the final result passes 360:00, subtract 360:00.
   NOW YOU HAVE CHANGED THE PLACE.
4. In the Dalton Table of Houses, find the R.A. that is nearest your answer and take all the cusps but the MC for the chart; use the birth Lat. as usual. The difference between the R.A. you worked and the one in Dalton's that is nearest-&-LESS is minutes to add to the M.C. accompanying that lesser R. A. (For S. Latitude, this is the I.C., not the M.C.) Use the calculated natal planets if you have them but otherwise take the planets from the ephemeris.

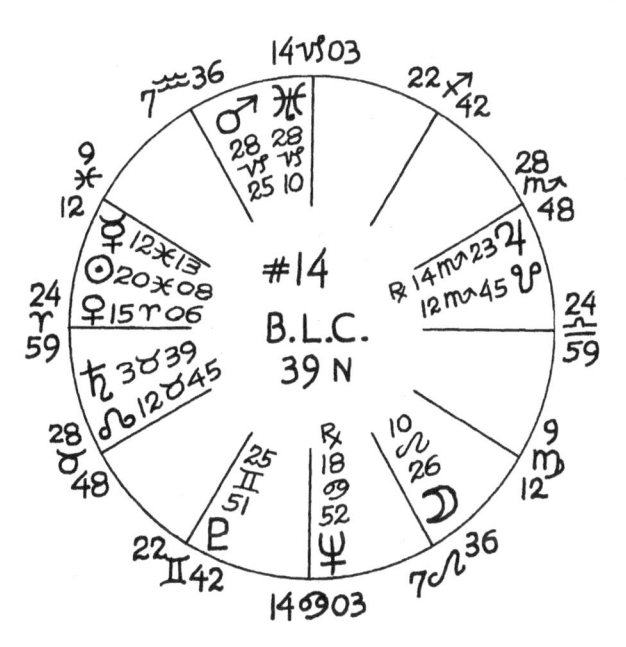

A Birth Locality Chart 75

March 11 1911 .... SUN Pisces 20 = 350:48
94:36-W 39-N   08 /   :08
(Jean Harlow)   R. A. Sun 350:56

```
                    14 ♑ 03
           7 ♒ 36      ♂ ♓       22 ♐ 42
        9 ♓                28 28
        12                 ♑ ♑       28 ♏ 48
                           25 10
     24 ☿ 12 ✶ 13
     ♈   ⊙ 20 ♓ 08          #14        ℞ 14 ♏ 23 ♃
     59  ♀ 15 ♈ 06          B.L.C.       12 ♏ 45 ♘    24 ♎ 59
                            39 N
           ♄ 3 ♉ 39
          ☊ 12 ♉ 45
      28 ♉ 48                                       9 ♍ 12
              25 ℞           10
              ♊ 18           ♌ 26
              51 ♋           ☽
                 52
         22 ♊ 42   ♇    ♆        7 ♌ 36
                    14 ♋ 03
```

                                    3   2   1

Line 1 ....   29:10 RAMC Grn Mch 21, 1930
                                 -    :15 minus Dif before 1930
                               28:56 RAMC Grn Mch 21, 1911
1930 Base Year   / 350:56 RA/Sun March 11, 1911
-1911 Birth Year   379:51 Perm/RAMC Grn 3/11/11
   19 Yrs = 15' Diff.

                             - 94W36 Birth Longit (/E, -W)
                              285:15 RAMC Birth Loc. Chart
                           - 285:12 Near-&-Less = 14 Cap.
                                 :03 03

A Locality Chart & its Placidian Arc

A Locality Chart other than for the birthplace can be set, disclosing what to expect if the native identifies himself with other localities by living there. It is not a permanent chart like the BIRTH Locality Chart or a natal chart: those two are lifelong, even though the native leaves his place of birth. A Locality Chart is good only while the "visitor" remains there, but it is extraordinary in its power to reveal the person's life and opportunities as well as his misfortunes if any in that locality.

It is therefore the part of wisdom to set a Locality Chart before committing yourself to a definite removal from what may be a better environment.

Go back to the Permanent R.A. of the Midheaven as on page 75 for the BIRTH Locality Chart for Jean Harlow in Kansas City, Mo. and take her away from her birthplace by substituting the Longitude for Los Angeles 118:15-W where she gained fame and fortune.

The Permanent RAMC plus or minus the Longitude of the new locality gives the RAMC for the Locality Chart, as follows:
```
    379:51  Permanent RAMC Greenwich
   -118W15  Longitude L.A. (≠E, -W)
    261:36  RAMC for L.A. Locality Chart
   -261:17  Nearest-&-Less = MC 22 Sag.
       :19 ................... 19
```

To show the cusps and transits for any special event we "Direct the wheel on a Placidian Arc" as explained on page 77, for an event occurring on June 7, 1937.

Directing on a Placidian Arc

The Placidian Arc (named for Plácidus) is simply the position of the transiting Sun changed to Right Ascension for this work (see page 74). To direct the chart to a special day, add the RA/Sun on that day to the RA of the M.C. that gave the Locality Chart, thus finding the progressed cusps by "Directing on a Placidian Arc".

This is Jean Harlow's Locality Chart for Los Angeles where she died on June 7, 1937 when the transiting Sun was in Gemini 16:18, his R.A. being 75:05.

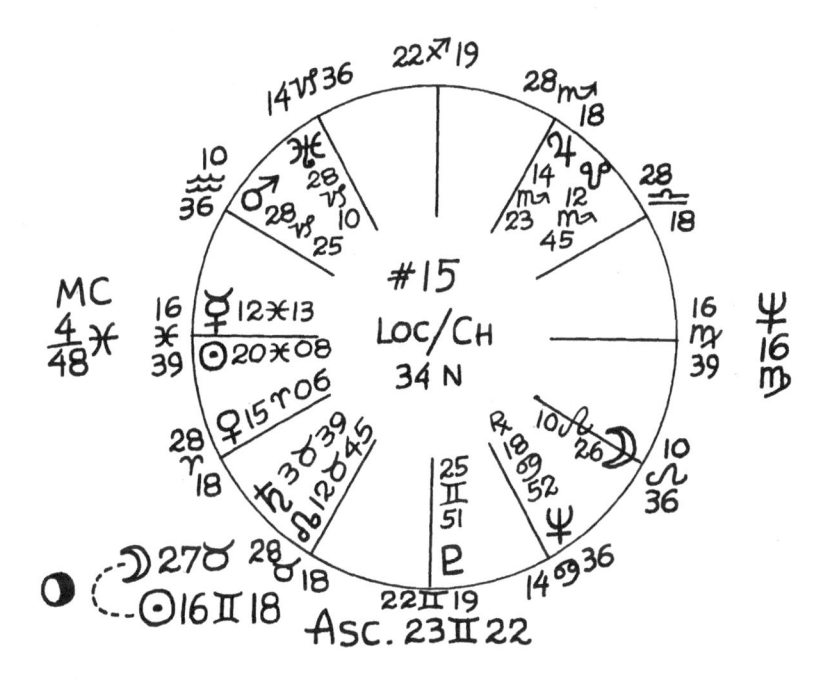

```
     261:36 RAMC Loc/Chart              Sun square ASC
   + 75:05 RA/Sun 6/7/'37               Neptune opp. ASC
     336:41 RAMC at death               ASC conjunct LC.
    -335:53 Directed MC 4:48 Pisces ..... sesquare Neptune
```

Johndro WORLD Charts

A World Chart is a wheel (cusps only) set for a place instead of a person, and always for March 21st of any year. Because of its slow motion of only 46.10 seconds per year it does not change appreciably in a lifetime. It is a wheel waiting for something to happen and when something DOES we note the transits that day and where they fall in the chart to make the locality register in the world news that day. The Placidian arc (R.A. Sun) gives us the directed cusps for that day (see p. 77). We use the same method as given on p. 74 but omit Step 2 because we are not changing the date from March 21st.

The World Chart for the Republic of Israel (Tel Aviv, 34:46 East & 32:04 North) is figured in Example #1 and shown on page 79. Whenever Israel registers in world news, that day's transits will register in this wheel. Also, strong transits falling in the angular houses of this wheel will bring Israel to wide notice. Tel Aviv was "born" at 4:06:00 p.m. E. European Time, May 14th, 1948, with MC 26 Cancer, ASC 24 Libra, almost the same angles as in its Birth Locality Chart figured below in Example #2, demonstrating the value of Johndro charts.

Example #1	Example #2
29:10 RAMC Grn 3/21/1930	29:10 RAMC Grn 3/21/1930
∕ :14 (18 years after ")	∕ :14 (18 years after ")
29:24 RAMC Grn 3/21/1948	29:24 RAMC Grn 3/21/1948
(Omit R.A./Sun	∕ 15:16 RA/Sun May 14 1948
in World Charts)	80:40 Perm/RAMC Grn 1948
∕ 34E46 Tel Aviv (∕E, -W)	∕ 34E46 Tel Aviv (∕E, -W)
64:10 RAMC World Chart	115:26 RAMC B. L. Chart
-64:06 = M. C. 6 Gemini	-114:49 = M. C. 23 Cancer
:04 04	:37 37

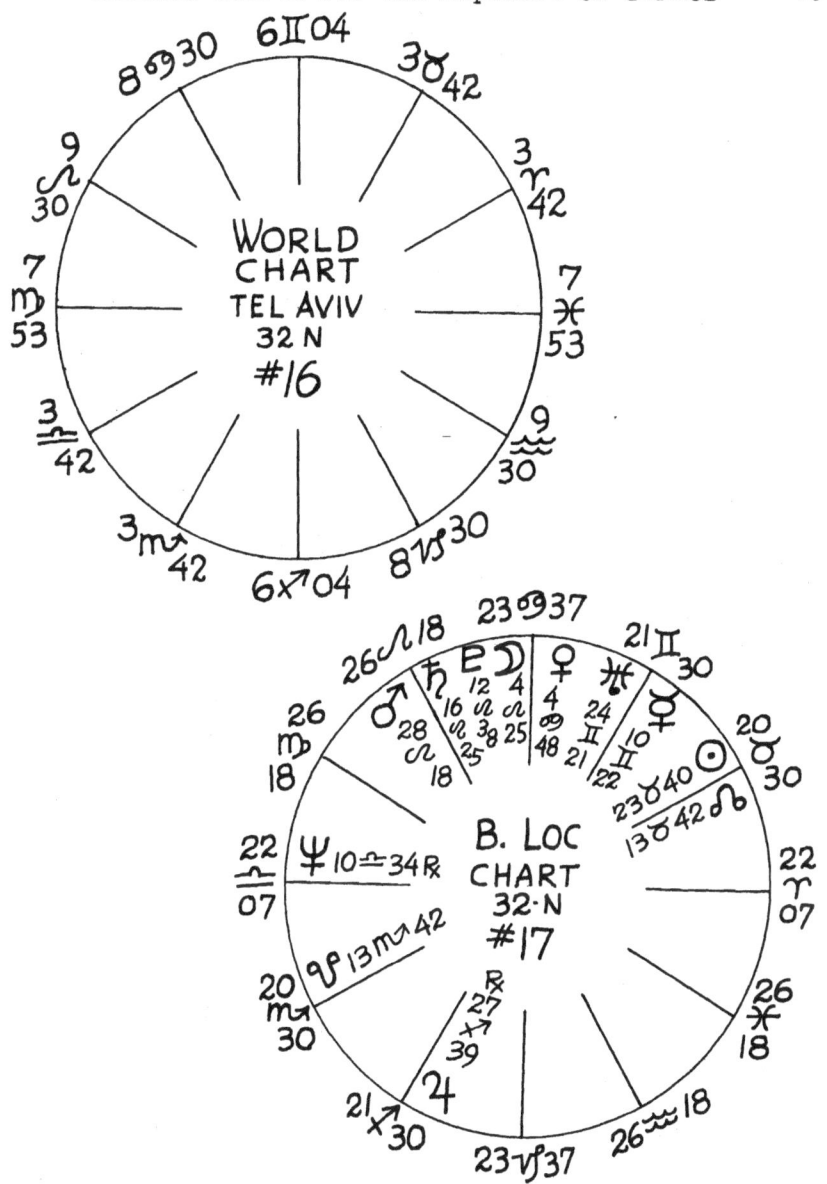

Johndro Charts for the Republic of Israel 79

WORLD CHART TEL AVIV 32 N #16

B. LOC CHART 32·N #17

The INGRESS Charts

Mundane Astrology deals with world conditions, which are HOUSE-rulership matters involving the stock market, foreign and domestic affairs, trade in general, labor, unions of all kinds, politics, vital statistics & war, to enumerate only a few.

The important charts are the four Ingresses or entry of the Sun into the Cardinal Signs Aries, Cancer, Libra and Capricorn. We want to know the day & hour it happens at Greenwich, so we can set up the LONDON Ingress Chart for world-wide conditions - thereafter adjusting it for our WASHINGTON Ingress Chart (national affairs) and for local ingress charts (home-town conditions).

1. Take the date when the Sun is nearest 0:00:00 of the required Sing: find the difference and, using the logarithm card, change it to the Log/Distance. Correct the minutes as in the example on page 81.
2. If the Sun was 0:00:00 of the Sign BEFORE noon of that date, find his motion between that date and the day before. If it happened AFTER noon of that date, find his motion between that date and the day after. Change the motion to Log/Motion.
3. The Log/Distance minus the Log/Motion gives the Log/Time (falling between a Greater & a Lesser). Change the Log/Time back to hours, min. and sec. to find D to add to the Lesser Time. Mark the result GMT/Interval.
4. If the Ingress occurred AFTER noon, ADD the GMT/Interval to 12:00:00 noon, mark it p.m. LMT, and change this to the Constant Log. If the Ingress occurred BEFORE noon, SUBTRACT the GMT/Interval from noon (11:59:60) & mark the result a.m. LMT. This GMT/Interval is to be changed to the C. Log.

London INGRESS Sept. 23, 1945

1. Sun Sept 23rd 0:05:17 Libra at noon
   Required Sign 0:00:00 Libra was BEFORE noon
   Difference ..   5:17 between 5' = 2.4594 log.
                        "   and 6' = 2.3802 log.
   A x C ÷ B = 224/D   17/C   60/B   792/A

   As the 5:17 minute increases, its log 2.4594 decreases
   and we are looking for the missing log between the two
   that gave us A. Using the 5' log 2.4594, minus 224/D
   because it is decreasing, to get   2.4370 Log/Distance

---

2. Sun Sept 23rd 00:05:17 Libra
   Sun Sept 22nd 29:06:34 Virgo
   Difference ..   58:43 between 58' = 1.3949 log.
                        "   and 59' = 1.3875 log.
   A x C ÷ B = 53/D   43/C   60/B   74/A

   We are again looking for the missing log between those
   that gave us A. Using the 58' log 1.3949 minus 53/D
   because it is decreasing, to get   1.3896 Log/Motion

---

3. 2.4370 Log/Distance
   -1.3896 Log/Motion
   1.0474 Log/Time ...... between 9' = 1.0478 log.
                            and 10' = 1.0444 log.
   1.0478 Log/Lesser Minute   60/B   34/A
   -1.0474 Log/Time
        4/C   2:09:00 = 1.0478 log
                               ∤ :07 = D
   B x C ÷ A = 7'/D   2:09:07 GMT/Interval

---

4. 11:59:60 Noon Sept. 23rd, 1945
   - 2:09:07 GMT/Int (BEFORE noon) ..... 1.0478 C. Log
     9:50:53 a.m. LMT Sept 23 1945
     " "   "   " Set London Ingress Chart for this time

FOUNDATION OF THE ASTROLOGICAL CHART

The Ingress other than for London.

Before we find the Ingress for other places, we work the London Chart and from it proceed elsewhere.

On page 81 we found the time of the Ingress (London) to be 9:50:53 a.m. LMT Sept. 23, 1945; GMT a.m. 23rd & 1.0478 the Constant Log.

```
   9:50:53 a.m. GMT Sept 23 1945         MOON 21:49 Aries
 +12:00:00 previous noon Sept 22
  21:50:53 Interval since noon           (MC: 27:00 Leo
      3:38 10-sec corr. Interval         (11, 29:00 Vir
 +12:03:56 Sidereal Time Sept 22         (12, 23:00 Lib
  33:58:27 more than 24 hours            (ASC 11:32 Sco
 -24:00:00 one sidereal day              (2d, 10:00 Sag
   9:58:27 Calculated Sid. Time .. 51N32 (3d, 18:00 Cap
```

We take the Calculated Sidereal Time from the London work and subtract the EGMT for West Longitude places – but add the EGMT for East Longitude places – giving us the Calculated Sidereal Time for the Ingress Chart for the other locality.

```
         9:58:27 Calc. S.T. for London
       - 5:08:00 EGMT Washington (-W)
         4:50:27 Calc. S.T. Washington
                      77-W, 39-N

         9:58:27 Calc. S.T. for London
       + 9:19:00 EGMT Todyo  (+E, -W)
        19:17:27 Calc. S. T. for Tokyo
                      140-E 36-N
```

Use the London Ingress planets for all other Ingresses.

An Ingress Chart

The Autumnal Equinox at Washington, D.C.

September 23, 1945

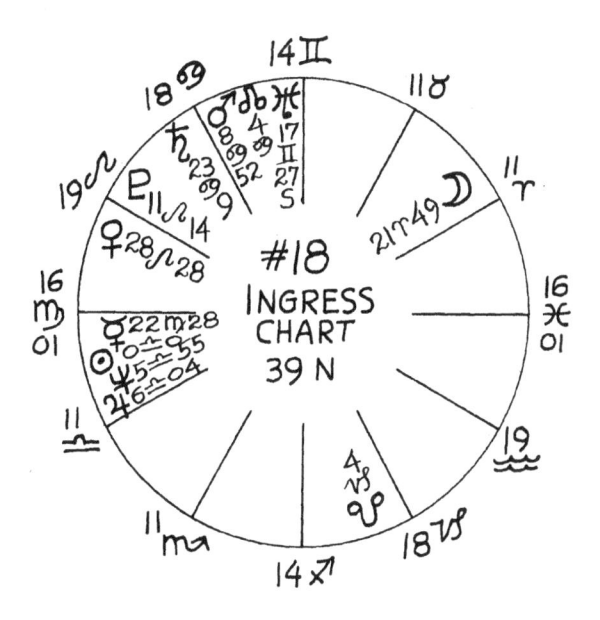

#18 INGRESS CHART 39 N

```
S u n       0:00 S        Venus    12:42 N
Neptune     1:06 S        Saturn   21:13 N
Jupiter     1:23 S        Uranus   22:52 N
M o o n     4:01 N        Pluto    23:13 N
Mercury     5:17 N        Mars     23:27 N
```

Always list the declination of the planets because the parallel of declination is an important aspect in Mundane Astrology, as strong as a conjunction. The Moon's declination should be calculated exactly, as on p. 31.

The International Date Line.

Relating itself to Prime Meridian 180:00 in the mid-Pacific is the International DATE Line or the midnight line where the date changes between two noons. One of these noons, say Monday, marks International Date Line EAST located at Wake Island in the North Pacific Ocean 12 hours east of Greenwich, using Meridian 180-E whose EGMT is therefore -12:00:00 later than Greenwich time.

The other noon, say Sunday, marks International Date Line WEST, located at the Wallis Islands in the South Pacific Ocean, 12 hours west of Greenwich, using 180-W whose EGMT is ⁄12:00:00 & earlier than Greenwich time.

```
Grn    EGMT -12:00:00      180      EGMT ⁄12:00:00      Grn
0-E                        E:W                          W-0
  :       Wake              :                            :
  :       166E35            :         Sunday:            :
  :         :               :           :                :
  :         :               :         Wallis             :
  :       :Monday           :         176W08             :
                     Date-Line Area
```

Since the EGMT is exactly 12 hours, localities using 180-E or 180-W need only mark their true clock time by the opposite term, a.m. or p.m., to find their GMT.

Wake Island	Wallis Islands
7:30:00 p.m. Std T. 2nd	7:30:00 a.m. Std T. 2nd
- 53:40 Diff W of 180-E	⁄ 15:28 Diff E of 180-W
6:36:20 p.m. LMT on 2nd	7:45:28 a.m. LMT on 2nd
⁄12:00:00 (to subtract)	⁄11:44:32 EGMT Wallis Is.
18:36:20 earlier than pm	19:30:00 later than a.m
-11:06:20 EGMT Wake Is.	-12:00:00 noon of the 2nd
7:30:00 a.m. GMT on 2nd	7:30:00 p.m. GMT on 2nd
from 11:60 = .7270 C. Log	= .5051 C. Log

The Antiscia or SOLSTICE POINTS

When the Sun's greatest distance from the Celestial Equator takes him north to 0-Cancer & south to 0-Capricorn (see diagram on p. 72) he apparently stands still (sol-stice) in turning back (ant-iscia) and emphasizes these two points accordingly, especially when referred to the planets, who revolve around him.

A planet's Solstice Point is its distance from 0-Cancer or 0-Capricorn, whichever is nearer, taken over to the other side of that solstice, and is extremely easy to figure. The planet's remaining degrees & minutes in the Sign it is in are the degrees and minutes for that planet's Solstice Point. The Sign to use is the one on the same line with it in the following diagram:

Capricorn	:	Sagittarius
Aquarius	:	Scorpio
Pisces	:	Libra
Aries	:	Virgo
Taurus	:	Leo
Gemini	:	Cancer

In Chart #8 repeated on page 49, the Sun's remaining degrees in Pisces (29:60 - 5:51) are 24:09 while Libra is on the same line, giving 24:09 Libra the Sun's S.Pt. This waits for a major progression or transit to reach it and galvanize it into action resulting in an event. At about age 30 the progressed Ascendant will conjunct his Solstice Point and activate it accordingly. The S.Pt for Mercury-ruler-Ascendant is 12:31 Scorpio & by age 30 (at the Sun's rate of a-degree-a-year) it will be conjunct Saturn in the 3rd House of travel, and the progressed Moon will be back in Capricorn trine Jupiter who rules his travel-3rd. We would therefore expect him to take a trip about that time.

How to Use the MIDNIGHT Ephemeris.

Where a noon ephemeris such as Raphael's begins each day's planet positions as at noon that day, a midnight ephemeris begins each day's planet positions as at midnight BEFORE noon that day.

Example: 7:34:00 a.m. PST Nov. 14, 1936, 118:15-W 34-N
(See example work on page 87)

1. RELATE THE BIRTHPLACE TO ITS NEAREST PRIME MERIDIAN (follow the same procedure as for Rule 1 on page 12) Also CHANGE THE CLOCK TIME TO LOCAL MEAN TIME (LMT) (follow the same procedure as for Rule 2 on page 12)

2. FIND THE INTERVAL (the time elapsed between the LMT & its preceding MIDNIGHT). An a.m. LMT *is* the time elapsed since midnight; mark it INTERVAL also. But a p.m. LMT is since noon so we have to add 12 hours to find the Interval since the preceding midnight.

3. CHANGE LONGITUDE TO TIME: call it the EGMT as usual

4. ADD THE 10-second CORRECTION FOR THE INTERVAL (Rule 5, p. 13) and for the EGMT if the Longitude is West.

5. ALWAYS ADD THE SIDEREAL TIME FOR THE DATE OF BIRTH.

6. Add 12:00:00 for South Latitude, but not otherwise. Start with the 4th cusp, then the 5th, and so on.

7. For East Longitude subtract the correction for EGMT

8. This gives the Calculated Sidereal Time for the cusp

7:34:00 a.m. PST Nov. 14, 1936, 118W15 34N   87

```
   7:34:00 a.m. PST Nov 14 1936
+  7:00      Diff. E. of 120:00 W        (MC:  .. 18:00 Vir
   7:41:00 a.m. LMT-Int. Nov 14          (11,  .. 18:42 Lib
   1:16   10-sec corr. for Int           (12,  .. 14:00 Sco
   1:18   10-sec  "    7:53 EGMT         (ASC  ..  5:39 Sag
+  3:31:40 Sid. Time, Nov. 14th          (2nd  ..  7:06 Cap
  11:15:14 Calculated S. Time .. 34N     (3rd  .. 12:30 Aqu
```

10. FIND THE GREENWICH MEAN TIME & Constant Logarithm.

   The LMT plus the EGMT equals the GMT
    for births in West Longitude.
   The LMT minus the EGMT equals the GMT
    for births in East Longitude.
   Mark the GMT a.m. or p.m. & date it.

   An a.m. GMT is changed at once to the
    C. Log (use the logarithm card).
   A p.m. GMT is subtracted from the com-
    ing midnight (call it 11:60) and
    the result changed to the C. Log.

Take the planets on the GMT date and the one following
and calculate as usual --- but for an a.m. GMT add the
small motion to the place on the GMT date. For a p.m.
GMT subtract it from the place on the following date.
(For a retrograde planet, do just the opposite.)

```
The GMT & Constant Log.                   Moon
    7:41 a.m. LMT 14th
+   7:53 EGMT W-Longit       15th,  1:13 Sagittarius
   15:34                     14th, -19:19 Scorpio
  -12:00 coming noon               11:54 = 3047 log.
    3:34 p.m. GMT 14th           + 4542        C.L.
om 11:60 midnight 14th       15th, -4:11 = 7589 log.
    8:26 = 4542 C. Log             27:02 Scorpio
```

The Terms of the Planets

The ancient Egyptians recognized seven celestial bodies as the "Seven Powers before the Throne" which were the Sun, Moon, Saturn, Jupiter, Mars, Venus & Mercury. Of these, they considered various areas in the Signs to respond to the nature of the five planets as listed in the following Table. The degrees given are inclusive.

The Egyptian Table of Terms

Aries	- Jup	6	Ven	12	Merc	20	Mars	25	Sat 30
Taurus	- Ven	8	Merc	14	Jup	22	Sat	27	Mars 30
Gemini	- Merc	6	Jup	12	Ven	17	Mars	24	Sat 30
Cancer	- Mars	7	Ven	13	Merc	19	Jup	26	Sat 30
Leo	- Jup	6	Ven	11	Sat	18	Merc	24	Mars 30
Virgo	- Merc	6	Ven	17	Jup	21	Mars	28	Sat 30
Libra	- Sat	6	Merc	14	Jup	21	Ven	28	Mars 30
Scorp.	- Mars	7	Ven	11	Merc	19	Jup	24	Sat 30
Sagit.	- Jup	12	Ven	17	Merc	21	Sat	26	Mars 30
Capri.	- Merc	7	Jup	14	Ven	22	Sat	26	Mars 30
Aquar.	- Merc	7	Ven	13	Jup	20	Mars	25	Sat 30
Pisces	- Ven	12	Jup	16	Merc	19	Mars	28	Sat 30

The Ascendant or any planet in the above areas takes on the nature of the planet characterising that area & assists the astrologer in reading the native's type of response or reaction accordingly. Mars vibrations are enterprising, Venus artistic, obedient and benevolent; Mercury, clever and vocally expressive; Jupiter, aware of ceremony and authority; religious; Saturn, profound and tactful, conscientious in expressing the planet.

In Chart #14, p. 75, Jean Harlow's artistic Venus in the Mercury area has aptitude with the spoken word.

The DIURNAL Chart

The Diurnal Chart is a one-day TRANSIT chart set for a person as though he were born that day, therefore we combine his original birth time, latitude & longitude, with the date from the CURRENT ephemeris. Work only the Moon & any fast planet changing Signs, and use the original Constant Log.

During those years in which the regular progressions signify activity confirmed by the month-by-month Moon, we want to narrow down the probable day of the activity to a specific date or diurnal transit. That specific date will usually coincide approximately with a strong lunation (New or Full Moon) that aspects the Ascendant in the natal chart - but it must also conjunct a natal or progressed planet to cause an event. In this work, the Full Moon is apparently the more potent one.

Using Chart #13, p. 71, this man's regular progressed year 1956 brought Mercury to 13 Pisces square to Venus. It would be important because Mercury rules an angle - the family-4th: it would be unfortunate because of his Sign position (in his fall in Pisces): it would be unhappy and a loss because of the square to Venus, and as she is in the 6th it would involve an illness - but not his own, since the progressed Mercury does not afflict the Ascendant. It affects someone in the family because he rules the family-4th, and that is the house to read in the Diurnal Chart. This is our method of reasoning.

The steps to take

Starting with the confirming month-by-month Moon, we take this man's January when she also was in 13 Pisces siding with progressed Mercury against Venus. She had been in 13 Pisces before but not conjunct a progressed or natal planet: that makes the difference this time.

The Diurnal Chart, cont'd

Taking the 1956 ephemeris, we begin with the birthday in January and go forward through as many months as we need to in order to find a lunation that squares or opposes the Ascendant, bringing action into his circle & involving him unhappily to agree with the progression.

January showed no lunation afflicting the Ascendant. The New Moon in February did not aspect the Ascendant; the Full Moon did (6 Virgo) but the sextile is not afflictive. The New Moon in March did not aspect the Ascendant but the Full Moon in 6 Libra did, and by square so that he was personally affected and unhappily so.

This was on March 26th, but no progressed planet was there aspecting the Ascendant: this is the lunation to tie to therefore, but not the date for it to register. We must wait for the Moon to move on until she meets a planet that does aspect the Ascendant and this she did two days later, March 28th, when she came conjunct the progressed Mars in 6 Scorpio and sextile the natal Saturn in 11 Virgo. These are malefics, one ruling the death-8th House naturally & the other ruling it in the natal chart, revealing that the illness of a member of the family would result in death. It would not be his death because these two do not afflict the Ascendant.

We accordingly set the Diurnal Chart for the place & time of birth (87W19 38N46 and 3:40:44 pm/LMT) but the current date March 28, 1956. Since we originally took the Moon for the birthdate and the day after, we took her this time for the transit date and the day after, & we used the original Constant Log. 4025. All of this gave us the Diurnal Chart on page 91, opposite.

A Diurnal Chart

Related to Chart #13, p. 71

3:40:44 pm/LMT
March 28, 1956

87W19, 38N46
Family Death

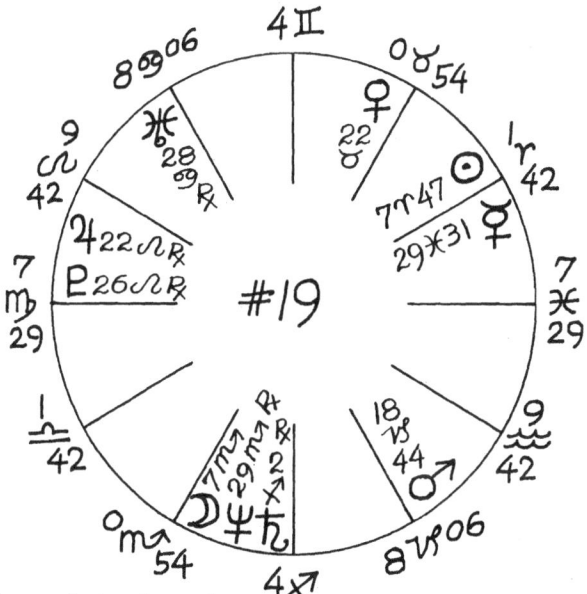

Since the original indication came from the progressed Mercury who rules the natal 4th, we look to the 4th in the Diurnal Chart for the basis of the event.

Jupiter rules the 4th and is in the 12th (misfortune and grief) and is square to Neptune (funerals) exactly sesquare to the Sun in the 8th (deaths in his circle), and exactly square to Venus (a loss greater than otherwise: one that cannot be replaced): a death.

For confirmation of death of the mother, the nearest planet to the 8th cusp is Mercury-ruler-10th (mother), & Mars-ruler-8th is in the death-8th from the 10th.

FOUNDATION OF THE ASTROLOGICAL CHART

The Adjusted Calculation Date

Instead of calculating the places of your progressed planets each year and beginning with your birthday, we may take the planets unworked and as given in the natal ephemeris & consider that they start operating on what is called the Adjusted Calculation Date. This may turn out to be before or after your real birthdate. Once ascertained, you keep the same A.C.D. throughout life.

The GMT-line and Birth Sidereal Time

Set up the chart as usual, but NOTE THE GMT-LINE AND THE BIRTH SIDEREAL TIME that you used.

RULE:

1. The INTERVAL from the GMT forward to the next noon, (corrected as per Step 5 on p. 13 herein) Plus the Birth Sidereal Time (not the Calc. S. T.), Gives the Sidereal Time for the A.C.D. (the ACD/ST)

2. If the GMT-hour is BEFORE noon of the date of birth (a.m. of the birthdate or p.m. of the previous day) Look FORWARD in the natal ephemeris to find the S.T. that is nearest the ACD/ST.

3. If the GMT-hour is AFTER noon of the date of birth, (p.m. of the birthdate or a.m. of the following day) Look BACKWARD in the natal ephemeris to find the S.T. that is nearest the ACD/ST.

4. The DATE accompanying the Sidereal Time nearest the ACD/ST is the Adjusted Calc. Date for your planets. On that date each year instead of your regular date your unworked progressed planets start operating.

The A.C.D., cont'd

Always write down your A.C.D. with other data on the natal chart-sheet for ready reference each year. (The A.C.D. is also known as the Limiting Date.)

For births occurring at the very beginning or end of the year, the ephemeris for the adjoining year may have to be used in going forward or backward from the birth date, as in Rules 2 and 3.

Example No. 1

```
  6:45 a.m. GMT June 13, 1903
  5:18:33 Birth Sidereal Time

 11:60:00 (12 hours to noon)
- 6:45:00 a.m. GMT June 13th
  5:15:00 uncorrected Int.
+    0:52 correction for Int.
  5:15:52 corrected Interval
+ 5:18:33 Birth Sidereal Time
 10:34:25 ACD/ST = Aug 31 ACD
```

Example No. 2

```
  1:46 p.m. GMT Sept 11, 1903
 11:13:23 Birth Sidereal Time

 23:60:00 (24 hours to noon)
- 1:46:00 p.m. GMT Sept 11th
 22:14:00 uncorrected Int.
+    3:42 correction for Int.
 22:17:42 corrected Interval
+11:13:23 Birth Sidereal Time
 33:31:05 (subtract 24 hours)
  9:31:05 ACD/ST = Aug 15 ACD
```

The Arabian Points & their use

The Arabian Points (PARTS) have to do with arithmetical degrees arrived at as we do with the Part (Point) of Fortune, where we use the Ascendant plus the Moon & then minus the Sun. The next most-commonly-used Parts are the following, applied to Chart #7 on page 27.

```
            Ascendant       9  23:05
          ⚹ the 7th         3  23:05
                           13  16:10
           - Venus           6   1:17
(M) Part of Marriage       (7) 14:53  Scorpio conj M.C.
```

The Part of Marriage conjunct the Midheaven promises a fortunate marriage, probably around age 17, when the Moon ruler-marriage-7th conjuncts (M) and then the Sun while the progressed (M) at the degree-for-a-year rate reaches 1 Sagittarius and sextiles Venus in Libra, the marriage planet in the marriage Sign.

Note that we must confirm our reading by several additional & appropriate progressed indications.

```
            Ascendant       9  23:05
          ⚹ the 8th         5   4:54
                           14  27:59
           - Moon           0  17:37
(D)  Part of Deaths        (2) 10:22  Gemini trine Saturn
```

At age 10, progressed Mercury-ruler-death-8th opposition (D) from 10:22 Sagittarius denotes a loss in the family circle (being then in the 11th, which is the 8th from the family-4th). The progressed Moon will be exactly conjunct (D) and trine Saturn in the 8th. The progressed (D) in 20 Gemini will trine Neptune (coma).

The Arabian Points, cont'd

The Part of Sickness (S)

The Ascendant plus Mars (acute) & then minus Saturn, (chronic) gives 4:54 Capricorn as the Part of Sickness (S) for Chart #7. This is semisextile Mercury, ruler of the sickness-6th; a weak aspect and a minor planet, denoting little more than a simple ailment. The first such illness would occur at age 6 because 6 days after birth (denoting years) the progressed Moon would be in the 6th House in opposition to (S) and setting off its aspect to Mercury, while the Ascendant in 29 Capricorn would exactly quincunx the 6th cusp as confirmation.

```
            Ascendant        9  23:05
        ⨍ ruler 8th          8  04:14  Mercury
                            17  27:19
          - Saturn            6  10:33
(P) The Part of Peril       11) 16:46  Pisces
```

The Part of Peril warns of dangers that are of major proportions if the Part is conjunct the Ascendant & in square to malefics at birth; otherwise, it is minor in comparison. If Capricorn is on the 8th cusp, the Part of Peril will be exactly conjunct the Ascendant, since we would plus and minus the same planet (Saturn) leaving the Ascendant itself in danger. In succeedent and cadent houses, the Part of Peril is less powerful than when angular. 8 days (years) following birth, Mercury ruler 8th (injury) squares (P) from 16 Sagittarius but the succeedent-house placement reduces a severe injury to merely a probable mishap.

The Part of Legacies (L)

The Ascendant plus the Moon, minus Saturn, gives the Part of Legacies (L) 00:09 Leo for Chart #7, promising a legacy because sextile Venus in the legacy-8th House.

The Life Cycle Chart

A special chart showing the event periods in the life is of great value in forecasting, particularly the one based on the "Life Cycle" work by Glahn, E. Baktay and others. We present such a chart on p. 97, founded on Chart #13, p. 71. Note Uranus now in the surgery-8th.

The natal Ascendant gives the Life Cycle Ascendant & the degrees for the remaining cusps with the Signs following in their natural order. Each quadrant measures 25 years of life, each house 8 years and 4 months, and each of the four sections in each house 2 years 1 month. (Add 8 degrees, then 7 and 7 as in the 1st House here.) The accumulation of 12 months gives an added year, and moves January forward 3 years and 1 month instead.

Starting with the month & year of birth, the Ascendant moves CONVERSELY toward the Midheaven. In going through the sections it indicates the year in which it sets off the aspects it makes to natal planets according to the degrees accompanying that year. We require at least two additional aspects to confirm the forecast and any major event must be promised at birth by natal planets: NO PROMISE MADE, NO PROMISE KEPT.

Chart #20, p. 97, shows the Ascendant in 8 Cancer as at the birth month and year, January 1920. As a child of 7, this man underwent a tonsillectomy. The Ascendant that year, 1927, was in the 1926/27 section in the hospitalization-12th in Gemini opposition Venus in the illness-6th, the planet ruling the tonsils. The Moon, ruler Ascendant, by Secondary progression in 29 Aquarius, was conjunct Uranus in the surgery-8th. The surgery planet Mars was sextiled by Venus 23 Sagittarius while squared by Mercury, ruler 12th in 23 Capricorn.

Life Cycle Chart based on Chart #13, p. 71   97

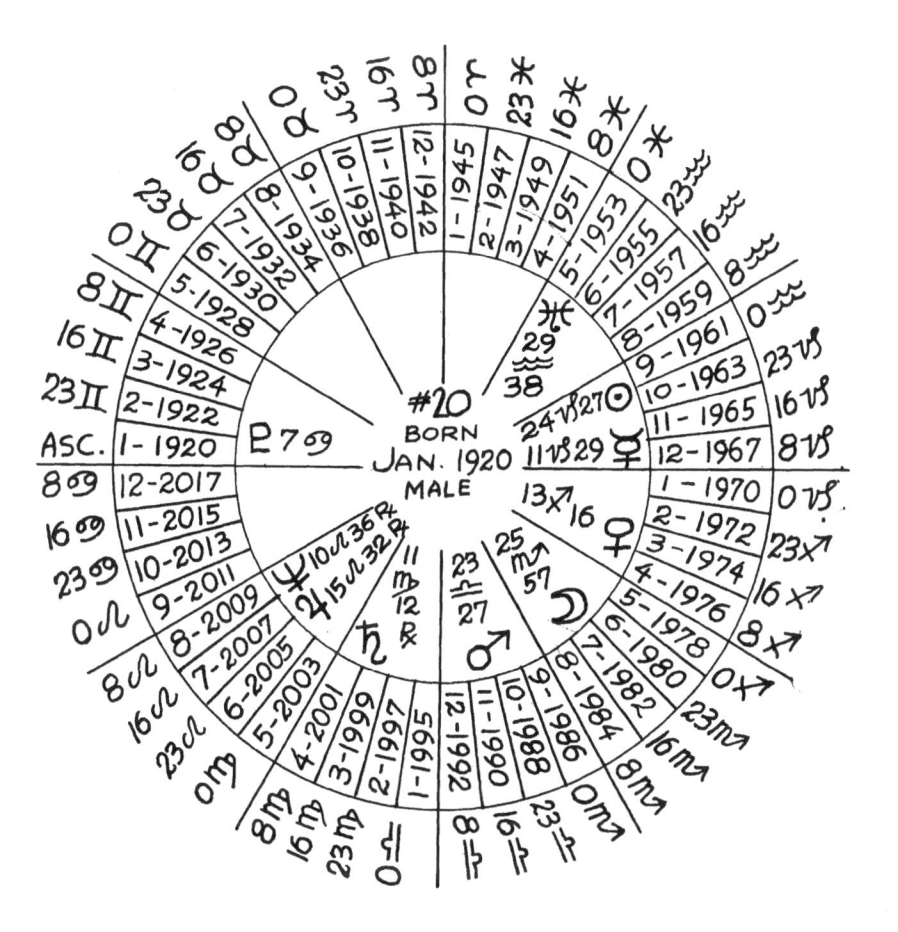

1939 — **Appendectomy.** Ascendant 23 Aries opposing Mars.
    Moon-ruler-Asc. 23 Leo sextile surgical Mars.
1942 — **Married.** Asc. 15 Aries trine to ritual-Jupiter.
    Moon conjunct Saturn, ruler of marriage-7th.
1956 — **Death of mother.** Asc. 25 Aquarius square Moon.
    Moon & Mercury 13 Pisces sq. Venus-ruler-4th.

PLANETARY DAYS & HOURS

The planet ruling the day itself rules the first hour of sunrise - somewhat earlier than 6:00 a.m. in summer & later than 6:00 a.m. in winter, therefore adjust the following list accordingly. Note the order of planets.

	☉	♀	☿	☽	♄	♃	♂
			1:am	2:00	3:00	4:00	5:00
SUN -	6:am	7:00	8:00	9:00	10:00	11:00	12:-N
☉	1:pm	2:00	3:00	4:00	5:00	6:pm	7:00
	8:pm	9:00	10:00	11:00	12:-M		
						1:am	2:00
MON -	3:am	4:00	5:00	6:am	7:00	8:00	9:00
☽	10:am	11:00	12:-N	1:pm	2:00	3:00	4:00
	5:pm	6:pm	7:00	8:00	9:00	10:00	11:00
	12:-M						
		1:am	2:00	3:00	4:00	5:00	6:am
TUE -	7:am	8:00	9:00	10:00	11:00	12:-N	1:pm
♂	2:pm	3:00	4:00	5:00	6:pm	7:00	8:00
	9:pm	10:00	11:00	12:-M			
					1:am	2:00	3:00
WED -	4:am	5:00	6:am	7:00	8:00	9:00	10:00
☿	11:am	12:-N	1:pm	2:00	3:00	4:00	5:00
	6:pm	7:00	8:00	9:00	10:00	11:00	12:-M
THUR -	1:am	2:00	3:00	4:00	5:00	6:am	7:00
♃	8:am	9:00	10:00	11:00	12:-N	1:pm	2:00
	3:pm	4:00	5:00	6:pm	7:00	8:00	9:00
	10:pm	11:00	12:-M				
				1:am	2:00	3:00	4:00
FRI -	5:am	6:am	7:00	8:00	9:00	10:00	11:00
♀	12:-N	1:pm	2:00	3:00	4:00	5:00	6:pm
	7:pm	8:00	9:00	10:00	11:00	12:-M	
							1:am
SAT -	2:am	3:00	4:00	5:00	6:am	7:00	8:00
♄	9:am	10:00	11:00	12:-N	1:pm	2:00	3:00
	4:pm	5:00	6:pm	7:00	8:00	9:00	10:00
	11:pm	12:-M					

QUESTIONS

FOUNDATION OF THE ASTROLOGICAL CHART

Page

Questions

1 - What is the difference between a constellation and a Sign? Name the 12 Constellations that form our Zodiac. What element is the 11th constellation, what does the pitcher pour and what does the Sign represent?

Answers

A constellation is a group of stars; a Sign is a mathematical unit of 30 degrees. The Ram, Bull, Twins, Crab, Lion, Virgin, Scales, Scorpion (also known as the Eagle or Swan in South Latitude), the Archer, Goat, Pitcher-Bearer, and the Fishes. The 11th is an AIR Sign, pouring the ethers (the space-filling medium air, not water), which flows in both directions as shown by the wavy lines in the symbol. It heralds the Brotherhood of Man.

What is Sidereal Time? Which fixed star sets the Sidereal Time? What is the ecliptic? What is a planet and how many are there? Are the Sun and Moon planets? Are they ever retrograde in motion?

2 - Name the angles of the chart by name, by position of the Sun, by clock time and by direction.

The Ascendant, Sunrise, 6:00 a.m. and EAST
The Zenith or Midheaven, 12:00 Noon, SOUTH
The Descendant, Sunset, 6:00 p.m. and WEST
The Nadir or 4th, 12:00 Midnight and NORTH

Which line marks the Horizon & which the Meridian? What are the Directions based on? Where do we in the Northern Hemisphere look to see the Sun at his highest, at noon? In the Southern Hemisphere?

Questions

3 - What divides the wheel into quadrants? What part marks the limits of our solar system? What do we call the Sun's path? Explain the difference between the Earth and the WORLD. How many houses are there, & why are they not all the same width? What is the Celestial Equator? Is it parallel to the Ecliptic? What is the deviation called? (See diagram on p. 72 for the deviation.) Which houses are diurnal & which nocturnal? Which are angular? Succeedent? Cadent?

4 - Name the 12 Signs of the Zodiac. How many degrees in each Sign? In the whole circle? Which Signs are masculine & positive? Feminine & negative? Which are Cardinal? Fixed? Common or Adaptable? Which start things going? Which take root & thus establish themselves? Which adjust themselves to existing conditions?

Name the Fire Signs, Earth Signs, Air Signs & the Water Signs. Which are intellectual? Emotional? Practical? Spiritual?

5 - Name each celestial body and the Sign in which it is dignified, detrimented, exalted & in its fall. They "rule" the Sign in which they are dignified. What does the Sun rule? The Moon? Where is Mars exalted? Is Saturn strong or weak in Aries and Libra? Which Sign is co-ruled by Uranus? Pluto? Neptune?

Which celestial body has the greatest speed? The least? Which is the fastest PLANET? How long is the Moon in a Sign? The Sun? Mercury, Venus and Mars are often retrograde, making them variable.& affecting the length of their stay in a Sign.

Questions

7 - How many wheels combine to form the Chart? What do they represent? On what date does the astrological year begin, and what is its other name?

> March 21st, the Vernal Equinox when the Sun crosses the Celestial Equator at 0-Aries on his way north to 0-Cancer, on the 4th cusp, which marks the Summer Solstice.
>
> This is not a contradiction in direction as the Sun is fixed and it is the Earth that is turning, bringing the North 4th cusp to him. Study the diagram on page 72.

What distinguishes the date June 21st? Where does it occur by Sign? What happens on September 21st and what do we call it? Where and when does the Winter Solstice occur?

How many hours to a house? Where do they fall? Where does the Sun ascend? Descend? When does a planet rise? Culminate? Set? What causes it?

8 - What is geographical Latitude? What do we mean by parallels of Latitude? How many are there? What tells us whether they are North or South? They are one degree apart, accounting for the fact that there are 180 of them, the distance between Poles. What is the Sun's greatest distance from the Celestial Equator and where does it fall?

> The Sun's greatest distance from the Celestial Equator is 23-deg 27-min which we call the Obliquity of the Ecliptic. It falls on his solstice dates, June 21st in 0-Cancer & December 21st in 0-Capricorn.

Questions

9 - What is geographical Longitude, where does it begin, what do we call the circles marking it & how far apart are they? How many are there?

> Geographical Longitude is distance on Earth beginning at 0-degrees located at Greenwich and marked by circles called meridians, one degree apart. There are 360 of them - 180 in East Longitude & 180 in West Longitude.

10 - Of the 360 meridians how many are Prime Meridians? What time of day do they designate? Why is Greenwich, England important? How many hours between Prime Meridians? How many minutes? How many degrees of distance? How much time in one degree? What is a LOCAL Meridian? Where do we locate the Local Meridian for any specific locality?

11 - What is the Equivalent Greenwich Mean Time (EGMT) for Longitude 150 East and Longitude 150 West?

> 150 degrees from Greenwich corresponds to 10 hours EGMT in either direction, E or W.

Name the 4 Standard Time Zones in the U.S.A. What is clock time? What is Sidereal Time? Of what is it the equivalent, as shown in the ephemeris?

12 - How do we change Clock Time to Local Mean Time? Is the right side of a Prime Meridian its E. side or its W. side? How do we change difference in Degrees to difference in Time? (Multiply by 4')

13 - What is the Interval? When do we add 12 hours to find the Interval? How do we find its 10-sec correction?   How do we change Longitude to time?

Questions

14 - How do we find the birth Sidereal Time? What do we combine to find the Calculated Sidereal Time?

15 - What use do we make of the Calc. Sid. Time? When the chart is set for a locality in North Latitude which cusp do we start with? For South Latitude, which cusp do we start with? Which cusps do we accept as given, and which do we correct? How do we correct the minutes for the minor cusps?

16 - The longitude of a PLACE is its distance from 0-degrees on Earth. The longitude of a celestial body is its distance from 0-degrees of a Sign, as Venus in 3 Leo. Where do we find the longitude of the Sun, Moon and planets? For what time of day? How do we find the Greenwich Mean Time (GMT), and how do we find the Constant Logarithm? What must we always remember to do?

    Mark the GMT-line a.m. or p.m., date it and set down the Constant Log. underscored.

17 - What is the logarithm card, and how do we use it? Which celestial bodies must we always calculate? When do we equate the motion of the slow planets?

18 - In calculating a planet's place, which dates must we use? What tells us to plus or minus the small motion? Which date will we always use for this? Recite the procedure for calculating the place of a direct planet; for a retrograde planet.

19 - In subtracting planetary positions, what do we do when one is too small, as the Moon's place on the 27th from her place on the 28th on page 19? What does "S" signify? What is the direction & speed

Questions

of the Moon's Nodes? Where do we find the North Node's position? Where will the South Node be?

21 - What tells us where to enter a planet, Fortuna or the Nodes by house? In Chart #4, p. 21, why is Mercury between the Sun and the Midheaven?

22 - What is the formula for finding the Part of Fortune (also called Fortuna)? Always put down the <u>number</u> of the preceding Sign for Ascendant, Sun & Moon, and the <u>name</u> of the following Sign for Fortuna. Compare the work for Fortuna on page 22 and on page 26. What number do we use for Aries, in setting down the Ascendant, Sun & Moon? (0-Signs) Calculate Fortuna as shown in Chart #4, page 21.

23 - When will we surely have an intercepted Sign in a chart? How will we mark it? What happens to its opposite Sign?

> An intercepted Sign denotes INTERFERENCE in the person's affairs in that house, & matters held in ABEYANCE for awhile when there is a planet there (either at birth or later when entering by progression).

24 - In finding the Calc. Sid. Time for a chart set for SOUTH Latitude, what differences will we observe? Are we finding the 10th cusp or the 4th? We work the planets the same way for any Latitude.

26 - In finding the Calc. Sid. Time for a chart set for EAST Longitude, what differences will we observe? What is the rule for finding the GMT in this case? Having found the GMT and Constant Log., we follow the regular procedure in calculating the planets.

Page   Questions   107

27 - What is meant by "mutual reception"? (Two planets, each in the other's Dignity Sign.) It gives mutual freedom to come and go, helping the person whose chart it is to get out of what he gets into.

28 - What differences did we observe in this case? (It is for EAST Longitude, so we subtracted the correction for the EGMT in finding the Calc Sid Time; and we subtracted the EGMT itself, in finding the GMT. It is for SOUTH Latitude; we added 12 hours in finding the Calc Sid Time, which took us south of the equator so we started with the 4th cusp.)

29 - When do we have to have an Added Line, in finding the GMT? What does it always result in? (The opposite a.m. or p.m. on the GMT from the LMT.)

30 - What is the difference between the latitude of a locality and the latitude of a planet? Does the Sun have latitude? Do we calculate the planets' latitude? How is the Moon's latitude calculated?

    The greater the Moon's latitude, the more latitude or leeway the person allows himself in his actions. He has a healthy disregard for trivial rules & regulations and his scope of interests is much wider.

31 - What is declination? Which Signs are north of the Celestial Equator? How do we calculate the Moon's declination when it is increasing? Decreasing? When changing direction (crossing 0-degrees)?

32 - In correcting the Midheaven & Ascendant how do we find A? B? C? D? In adding D, which Midheaven and Ascendant do we use?

Questions

34 - What is a decanate? How many in a Sign? Can we have a Taurus decanate in the Sign Aries? Based on the Sun in a decanate how many types of individualities do we more-easily recognize? Is this an absolutely cut-and-dried, complete disclosure?

> No; only a clue. Each person is made up of individuality (Sun) combined with personality (Moon) & temperament (Ascendant, which blends the mental and physical). A synthesizing of the whole chart is necessary before the student can describe the person's complete entity.

35 - How many Faces in a decanate? In a Sign? How do we rate a chart with the majority of planets Positive? (The person is more independent & sure of himself; less easily imposed on.)

36 - What is an aspect? How many degrees in an opposition? When is an aspect partile and when is it platic? What do we mean by ORB? When is an aspect applying? Separating? When is it formed by mutual application?

37 - In reading an aspect in the natal chart, which of the two planets do we name first? Name the celestial bodies in the order of their speed.

38 - How many degrees do we allow for the conjunction? The sextile? Semisextile? Semisquare? Square? Does a conjunction always occur in the same Sign?

39 - How many degrees in a square? Trine? Sesquare? Quincunx? Is it easy to find the quincunx? (It shows where the person must reorganize his life.)

Questions

40 - How do we find the Parallel? What orb is allowed? The parallel resembles which other aspects? Name the five less commonly used aspects.

41 - What is the basic rule to figure the orb to allow? Is this procedure necessary? (No: the Table shows that we can allow an orb of 8 degrees for the conjunction, sextile, square, trine & opposition although the Sun and Moon may have 10 degrees. We recognize these as the strongest aspects. We allow 4 degrees for the semisquare and sesquare because they are related to the strong square. We allow 2 degrees for the semisextile, quintile and trecile, the biquintile and the quincunx. The semiquintile, nonogon & parallel are allowed 1.)

42 - What is a lunation? What is an eclipse, and when can a lunation be an eclipse? What is the symbol for an eclipse? (A half-blacked circle.) What is the ASPECT-symbol for a solar eclipse as shown in the list of lunar aspects in the ephemeris? For a lunar eclipse? Is the same eclipse seen all over the world? If not, how is it rated? What is an occultation? What is its symbol? Does the Moon make any aspect to Mars as listed on page 43?

43 - In the aspect list, which planets are descriptive of activity in the life? (Those showing many aspects, meaning many relationships to express.) In the Specimen Chart #9, p. 43, which planets denote an active life? (Those in angles: the 1st, 4th, 7th and 10th Houses.)

>A planet within five degrees of the next house cusp is considered to be operating in the next house also, as Mars here.

Questions

44 - What is the formula for finding a midpoint? Which midpoints do we calculate? When subtracting from a lesser Sign, what do we do?

45 - Which aspects do we list for the Moon in a Horary Chart? Where do we find the TABLE for her change to another Sign? Where is the ASPECTARIAN & what use do we make of it? Which aspect do we show in parenthesis and why?

> A horary chart is one set for the birth of a question instead of a person. We erect it for the time the question first took form, and we read it according to special rules to answer the question.

46 - What is the basis of the Secondary Method of Progression? Which ephemeris do we use? What do we find first? (The Prog. Date) Which Sid. Time do we use? How do we find the Increase? What do we do with it? What does the Prog. Sid. Time do for the cusps? How do we progress the planets?

47 - Why will we choose any particular year to progress the chart? (A progressed aspect is culminating.) How long does the progressed chart operate, & from what date? The progressed Moon's motion for one day gives her motion for one year; how do we find her motion for one month?

48 - How do we show the Moon's position month by month and why do we do it? (To time the aspects she is going to make) When did she conjunct NATAL Mars? When did she conjunct PROGRESSED Mars? (The interim period showed the beginning and ending of a development involving Mars.)

Questions   111

49 - How do we show where the month-by-month Moon will
     be operating in the chart? (We enter her symbol
     and Sign position outside the wheel, listing both
     starting and finishing degrees for the year.)

50 - How can we tell that the birth hour requires rec-
     tification? We always do it through the Midheaven
     but how? If the Midheaven is off-aspect by 1 de-
     gree (year) how many minutes is the birth time off
     and how do we know this? (By the Table of Houses
     which shows the M.C. by degree and its S. T. by 4
     minutes increase for each degree.) When we find
     the acceptable M.C. in the Table of Houses & take
     its Sid. Time, what use do we make of the latter?

51 - What events in life help to pinpoint the birthtime
     and which houses are most dependable? (Angular.)
     When it is the Ascendant's aspect that is not op-
     erating as it should (in point of timing) what do
     we do? (We always rectify through the Midheaven,
     so we look in the Table of Houses for the desired
     Ascendant, and it will be accompanied by the cor-
     rect Midheaven: we use this as on page 50.)

52 - Why is it important to note the years in which the
     planets turn either Direct or Retrograde? Which
     ephemeris do we use? Do we go forward or backward
     to find the planet? When does it register in life?
     What do we call the forward area? (The Progressed
     Area.) The backward area is the Pre-Natal Area.

53 - What are the Critical Degrees based on? Where do
     they fall in the Cardinal, Fixed and Common Signs?
     When do they register for life? For a year? For
     a month? They denote matters reaching a critical
     point or crisis in the person's life.

Questions

Name the most prominent malefic fixed stars, their Sign-positions and their effect. Which is the accursed Sign? (Scorpio, seen as a scorpion from the Northern Hemisphere. From the Southern Hemisphere, however, it is seen as an eagle or swan.) What is the effect of Caput Algol's power? (Decapitation, or simply "losing one's head".)

54 - What three advantages recommend the Radix System? What is the Major Arc & what is it based on? What is an arc? How do we direct the chart? (By adding the arc for Direct Directions; by subtracting the arc for Converse Directions.)

> RADIX means root, or the original chart and its arrangement of planets by house. Since we add the arc to everything, the cusps and planets only change their degree and Sign, not their position. The original design or arrangement is still as it was at birth.

56 - What is the Minor Arc based on? How do we find the Minor Moon? How do we find her position each month? For a person born February 24, 1957, what is the Minor Moon's position May 25, 1966?

```
                              S    dg mn
   1966 5 25   (9 yrs         3   28:35
   1957 2 24   (3 mos              3:18
      9 3  1 = (1 day               :02
   Minor Arc ........           4   1:55
 ∱ Natal Moon .....             9  12:03
                               13  13:58
   - 12 Signs .......          12
   Minor Moon 5/25/1966        1) 13:58 Taurus
```

Page   Questions   113

58 - What is the rate of progression per year by major
     arc? Per month? What orb is allowed for events
     to transpire? How is the Oblique Ascendant found?
     What is the formula for the Directional Fortuna &
     what is the formula for the Oblique Fortuna?

     The natal Fortuna plus the major arc gives
     the Directional Fortuna. The Oblique As-
     cendant plus the Directional Moon & minus
     Directional Sun gives the Oblique Fortuna.

59 - How do we find a planet's Converse position? How
     is the Converse Oblique Ascendant found? How do
     we find the Converse Minor Moon and her month-by-
     month converse position?

60 - What does Mundane mean? (Worldly: house affairs,
     and particularly the cusps of the houses.) What
     is the design formed by a parallel? What does the
     line represent in the chart? (The Meridian for the
     Meridian Parallel: the Horizon for the Horizontal
     Parallel.) How do we find the Meridian Parallel?
     The Horizontal Parallel? The Rapt Parallel?

61 - How do we find the Quadrate Parallel, and what is
     the design it forms? (A square.) How do we find
     the Directional Parallel? Can ANY planet achieve
     this aspect?   (No: only the Minor Moon.)

62 - The place where the orbit of a planet crosses the
     path of the Sun - similar to the Moon's contact -
     marks that planet's nodes. How much change do we
     note in the nodal points of the planets? What is
     their effect on natal planets? How long does the
     effect last with natal planets? (Through life.)
     With the progressed Sun & ruler Ascendant?

Questions

63 - What is a Solar Chart? Do we use degrees or natal planets? Do we do any calculating? What is the purpose of a Solar Chart? What makes it personal? Where do transits come from? Whom do they represent in the Solar Chart?

>Your natal planets were your mother's transits on the day of your birth.

64 - List the planets by their numbers, as in Table I. How do we find your present-age planet? How does it register in your life during its period? (According to its nature and what it represents.)

65 - Why will Mercury always be significant in the life of Mr. Nixon? What gave him prominence & promise at birth of gain in the future? When could his greatest opportunity be expected to develop?

>The OPPORTUNITY aspect is the sextile. When progressed Mercury makes the sextile to natal Jupiter the promise would be fulfilled as in 1952 when Mr. Nixon was elected Vice-President.

66 - What is a Solar RETURN Chart? Which ephemeris do we use? What data do we always use? (The natal LMT, date, Calculated Sidereal Time; Latitude and Longitude if the person is at his birth locality on his birthday; otherwise, the Latitude & Longitude of the locality he is in on his birthday.)

How do we find the Sidereal Time for the Solar Return cusps? How do we find the Solar LMT? What tells us whether this LMT is a.m. or p.m.? What gives us the date for this LMT? Where do we get

Page   Questions   115

the Constant Log? Which planets do we calculate?
Using only applying aspects, what orb is allowed?

67 - In finding the GMT, if you have to subtract 12:00
(see work on page 67), remember that it is always
12:00 midnight and the GMT will always be p.m. of
the earlier date: you are working backward. The
Sun in the Solar Return Chart must be more than it
was on the earlier date or less than on the later
date of the two you use.

69 - Study the four paragraphs separately, in relation
to Mr. Nixon's Return chart applied to his natal.
Which houses denote publicity? What is the difference financially between the 2nd & 8th Houses?
Which House rules credit & honor, his standing in
the community, his reputation? (10th) Which is
the House designed to keep matters quiet? (12th)
What holds matters in abeyance? (Interceptions)

70 - What do we mean by the Lunar Return? Which date
and Sign do we always start with? Why do we have
a Permanent Table for the Lunar Return and why is
the native 12 years older at each return coupling
the same month and Sign? Which ephemeris is used?
Do we read the returning Moon to the natal chart?
(No: it is the same as the natal Moon.) We read
the planets that accompany the returning Moon.

71 - What is the Lunar Constant? It is used with the
Minor Moons listed in the Table on p. 70, and can
be applied in either of two ways:

    1.   To find the exact degree of the Minor
        Moon at the time of a known event. We
        find the MONTH in the Permanent Table

Questions

and this tells us the SIGN the Minor
Moon will be in. The date of the
event minus the Lunar Constant tells
the DEGREE the Minor Moon will have.
Note that we already know the date of
the event.

2. On the other hand, if we are looking
forward to <u>find the date</u> of an event
when the Minor Moon will be making a
strong aspect to the natal chart, we
already know the Sign and degree she
will be in. The Minor Moon in the
Table tells us the month she will be
there. The difference between the
Moon's degree that month & the Lunar
Constant gives us the date that month
and the right-hand side of the Table
will give the age in years.

72 - What is a LOCALITY Chart? What makes it a BIRTH
Locality Chart? Do we use Sidereal Time? What
is Right Ascension? (Distance from 0-Aries, as
measured by the Sun's travel in his path.) Where
is it measured? (Where his position in the ecliptic would fall on the Celestial Equator. Thus we
have an equivalent: each degree in the Zodiac has
its equivalent in Right Ascension.)

What is an arc? What does the word ARC at the top
of the page in the Table of Houses refer to? (To
Right Ascension) What is it used for? (To find
the Midheaven) Do we work the planet-places? (If
we have a regular natal chart we take the planets
as worked; otherwise we use the planets unworked,
as given in the ephemeris for the date used.)

Questions

73 - How fast does the Midheaven progress per year? Is this enough to show any appreciable difference in a lifetime? (No: we use the age arc as given in the Table on p. 55, adding it to the Midheaven to find the progressed Midheaven. This we locate in the Table of Houses so that we can take the other cusps for the progressed Locality Chart.)

What is the specific use of the Correction Table, given on p.73? (To find the Difference to add or subtract in relation to 29:10 R.A.M.C. 1930 so as to have the R.A.M.C. for the year we wish to use.)

74 - What is the basic Right Ascension for the M.C., & what is the basic locality? For what date of what month? For what year? What is Line 1?

<u>29:10 RAMC Greenwich, March 21, 1930</u>
This is Line 1

How do we change the Sun's place to R.A.? If he has minutes, what do we do with them?

```
Sun Leo 14 = 136:28 R.A.
Minutes 21 /    :21
Sun ........ 136:49 R.A.
```

How many steps are required to change the Base to suit the individual whose chart it is? How do we change the year? The date? The locality? How do we find the minutes to put on the M.C.? What do we do for a chart for South Latitude? (We add 180:00 to find the 4th cusp instead of the 10th.) If the final result is more than 360:00 what must we do? Which planets do we use?

Questions

75 - What sort of chart is shown on page 75? (It is a locality chart that is a BIRTH Locality Chart because we added the R.A. of the Sun on the date of birth.) To progress it, we add the age arc as in the Table on page 55 to the Midheaven. For death on June 7, 1937, the age arc 25:52 progressed the Midheaven to 9:55 Aquarius. This brought the 4th cusp (end of life) to the conjunction of the Moon which rules the 4th, also to the exact semisquare of Pluto who co-rules the 8th House (death). This demonstrates the validity of the Johndro charts.

76 - What is the difference between a Birth Locality & just a Locality Chart? How long do the two last? How many locality charts may we set up? (As many as we wish.) What is the formula for finding the Midheaven for another locality? (Go back to the Permanent RAMC Greenwich and apply the longitude of the new locality: plus if East, minus if West.)

77 - What is a Placidian Arc? How do we find it? How do we use the Placidian Arc to find the cusps for any desired DAY of the year? What do we call this procedure? (Directing on a Placidian Arc.)

To which chart do we read these directions? (To either the Locality Chart or Birth Locality Chart as desired.) Which planets do we use? (Transits for the day under consideration.)

78 - What is a WORLD Chart? What date do we use? How does this figuring differ from that for the Birth Locality Chart? (Compare the World Chart for Tel Aviv, Example #1 with the Birth Locality Chart for Tel Aviv, Example #2.) How do we direct a World Chart? (On a Placidian Arc for a special day.)

Questions

79 - What is the difference between the two charts on page 79? Can we progress them?

Chart #16 is the locality's position in the world (an Equinox Chart as of March 21st) and is simply a framework to show transits on any desired day. Strong transits make the locality register in affairs of the world and in the news that day. The cusps may be directed by adding to the original RA of the MC (Example #1, p. 78) the RA of the Sun on the day of the strong transits.

Chart #17 is the Birth Chart for the Republic of Israel, in the same locality but made personal by one single and special birth date, so that it has "natal" planets. It is best progressed by applying the age arc to the Midheaven, as follows:

> For 1959, age 11 years, the age arc is 10:51 (see Table, page 55). This will bring the Midheaven to 4 Leo & conjunct the Moon in the 10th House. The Moon always inaugurates CHANGES and the 10th House has to do with POLICY. It will be a successful undertaking, since the Sun (SUCCESS) will be in 4 Gemini making the opportunity-aspect, a sextile, to the Moon who rules the policy-10th.

80 - What do we mean by mundane affairs? What is an Ingress Chart? Which must we always set up first (London) and what does it disclose? (WORLD conditions.) What does the Ingress Chart for a capital disclose? (NATIONAL conditions.) What does the Ingress Chart for a home town disclose? (LOCAL conditions.) How do we find the Log/Distance?

Questions

How do we find the Log/Motion? The Log/Time? The GMT/Interval? The LMT? The Constant Logarithm?

81 - In Step #1 and Step #2, the logs that give us "A" contain between them the missing log that we seek for the Log/Distance and the Log/Motion. We are working with the Sun & the Rule is A x C ÷ B = D. We always subtract D from the greater log.

In Step #3 the Rule is B x C ÷ A = D. We always add D to the time the logarithm card gives for the lesser log. This gives us the GMT/Interval, from which to find the LMT and Constant Log.

In Step #4 we find the LMT and Constant Log. If Step #1 shows 0:00:00 AFTER noon, we add the GMT/Interval to 12:00 noon, giving a p.m. LMT for the Ingress date; change this LMT to the Constant Log.

If Step #1 shows 0:00:00 BEFORE noon, change the GMT/Interval to the Constant Log. at once. Subtract the GMT/Interval from noon, which gives the LMT; mark it a.m. for the Ingress date.

82 - Which Ingress Chart do we work first? What do we start with? (The LMT we found on page 81.) What do we take from the London work for Ingress Charts elsewhere? (The Calc. Sid. Time) How do we find the Calc. Sid. Time for other localities? Which planets do we use?

83 - What is meant by an Ingress Chart for the Autumnal Equinox? (The Sun's entry into Libra.) What does an Ingress Chart for the Summer Solstice denote? (The Sun's entry into Cancer.) Why should we always list the declination of the planets?

Questions 121

84 - Where is the International Date Line? Which is its nearest Prime Meridian? What is its EGMT? For localities using 180E or 180W is it necessary to work the GMT? Why not? What do we do? (Mark the clock time for the opposite a.m. or p.m., and take the Constant Log. it gives.) When it is May 3rd at 180W what date is it at 180E? (May 4th)

85 - What is a planet's antiscia? (Its Solstice Point or distance from 0-Cancer or 0-Capricorn, whichever is nearer, taken to the other side of whichever solstice is used.) How do we find the degree and minute for the planet's Solstice Point? How do we know which Sign to use? What use do we make of the Solstice Points? (We note the aspects they make or receive by progression, disclosing a development in the person's affairs.) How do we progress a Solstice Point? (At the Sun's rate of approximately a degree a year.)

86 - In using the Midnight Ephemeris, which midnight do we use? (The midnight previous to noon.) How does the INTERVAL differ from our usual Interval? (It is the time elapsed since midnight, not since noon.) Which Sidereal Time do we always take?

87 - In using the Midnight Ephemeris, how do we change the GMT to the Constant Log? What happens to our Rule, that P.m. means plus, A.m. means minus? (We simply reverse it.)

88 - Which are the "Seven Powers before the Throne" and which celestial bodies rule the TERMS, or various areas in the Signs? In whose term does your Moon appear? Your Ascendant? Its ruler? What effect does this have on them?

Questions

89 - What is a DIURNAL Chart? Which ephemeris is used and what time, place & Constant Logarithm? Which planets do we calculate?

What is the purpose of having the Diurnal Chart & what does it give us? (It gives us a picture of a specific day and the transits then operating.) What is the main transit to work with? (A lunation that aspects the natal Ascendant while also conjoining a natal or progressed planet.)

What is our method of delineation? (We note an important progressed year and the Sign and degree of the most significant progressed planet. From the good or bad aspect it makes we interpret the effect in the natal chart.) The house it rules denotes the house to start with in the Diurnal Chart.

Starting with the month-by-month Moon we take the month in which she aspects the progressed planet, especially by conjunction, square or opposition.

90 - We use the CURRENT ephemeris, take the month just mentioned above, start with his day of the month, and go forward as many months as required to find a lunation that strongly aspects his Ascendant.

If that lunation also conjuncts a progressed or a natal planet, that is probably the day on which a development will take place. If it does not conjunct such a planet we must wait for it to do so, by moving forward to such a planet which does aspect the Ascendant. If the aspect is a good one, no harm comes to the person himself. However, we choose this date for the Diurnal Chart, combining it with the natal LMT, Latitude and Longitude.

Questions

91 - Why do we consider the 4th House the most important in reading this Diurnal Chart? What does the 12th House signify? Neptune not only rules funerals but is exactly opposition 29 Taurus, the place of the Pleiades (see page 53) also known as "The Weeping Sisters" and denoting when aspected that there is something to weep about. The square aspect signifies LOSS; when to Venus, Jupiter or the Sun (significators of gain) the loss is still greater. Which house represents the mother, and which is her death-8th? (The 10th and the 5th.)

92 - What is the Adjusted Calculation Date (also known as the Limiting Date) and what is its purpose? Do we find it more than once? What do we work with? (The GMT-line and the Birth Sidereal Time.) What are the rules? Which ephemeris do we use? Will the Adjusted Calculation Date be before or after the real birth date? Do we calculate the places of the progressed planets?

94 - Which is the most important Arabian Point or Part (the Part of Fortune) & what is its formula? Do we use the number of the Sign that the Ascendant, Moon & Sun are in? Why not? Why do we count off the number of the Sign in the answer and take the next Sign instead? What is the number for Aries?

What is the formula for the Part of Marriage, and what is this writer's symbol for it? What is the rate of progression for the Arabian Parts? (One degree equals one year.)

When a strong aspect is being made or received by the Part of Marriage does that assure a marriage? (Not unless it is confirmed by several additional

Questions

and appropriate progressed indications at the same time. These should include the marriage-7th cusp or a planet or point there, its ruler or Venus or Mars, and frequently Jupiter-of-rituals.) Otherwise it may indicate only a proposal of marriage.

What signifies death in the person's circle? Give the formula and symbol for the Part of Deaths.

95 - For the Part of Sickness, what is the formula and the symbol? Which planet shows acute afflictions and which denotes chronic disorders and ailments?

Give the formula and symbol for the Part of Peril and tell when it will always be exactly conjunct the Ascendant. When does it warn of major danger and when is it more minor in effect?

Give the formula and symbol for the Part of Legacies. Which House rules legacies & bequests, the possessions THE OTHER PERSON has to bestow? (8th) Which House rules inheritance? (The family-4th)

96 - Where do we find the Ascendant for the Life Cycle Chart? In which direction does the Ascendant progress? How many years in each quadrant? In each house? How many sections in each house?

How many years to a section? (2 years & 1 month, excepting for the December section which contains 3 years & 1 month.) What causes this? (The accumulation of the 12 months listed in the 12 sections to a quadrant amounts to another year before getting into January of the following year, so we add it to the last month in the year, December, & thus move January forward 3 years & 1 month after the year shown for December.)

Questions

Are the Life Cycle planets in the same houses as they are in the natal Chart? (Not always: sometimes they fall in an adjoining house, which will give an additional reading.

What is the effect of Uranus in the 8th House and squared by the Moon, ruler of the body-Ascendant? (The 8th rules surgery: the 8th Sign Scorpio also has to do with surgery: Mars rules knives & scalpels. Any aspect at all between the Moon & Mars, as in this chart, denotes surgery: a promise made to be kept.) Re-read the last paragraph, p. 96.

97 - Besides the tonsillectomy disclosed on page 96, & the appendectomy listed on page 97, this man sustained war injuries in 1950 resulting in lifelong paralysis, a bladder operation in 1952 and a year of corrective operations in 1955.

Take the 1920 ephemeris, find the progressed date for this man's age in 1950, 1952 and 1955, & take the progressed planets accounting for operations. Find the Life Cycle converse Ascendant by section and note its aspects to the natal planets in this chart. Why was 1955 so serious? What made these operations successful, nevertheless? (The aspect to surgery-Mars was the easy-success-TRINE.)

98 - Does the first hour of sunrise always register at 6:00 a.m.? Most newspapers give the exact rising and setting of the Sun for each day, together with the Moon. What is the ORDER of the planets? Name the days of the week and their planetary rulers. A Saturn hour is good for serious undertakings or dealing with older people: Moon, for dealing with the public: Mercury, for advertising: and so on.

*****